Mariatown to Maitland Ontario in Colour Photos, Saving Our History One Photo at a Time

Photography
by Barbara Raué
2016

Series Name:
Cruising Ontario

Book 155: Mariatown to Maitland
along the St. Lawrence River

Cover photo: Victorian house in Cardinal, Page 21

Series Name: Cruising Ontario
Saving Our History One Photo at a Time
in colour photos

Books Available in Alphabetical Order:
Aberfoyle, Acton, Alton, Amherstburg, Ancaster, Arthur, Aylmer, Ayr, Bloomingdale, Brantford, Burlington, Caledon, Caledonia, Cambridge, Clifford, Conestogo, Delhi, Dorchester to Aylmer, Drayton, Drumbo, Dundas, Eden Mills, Elmira, Elora, Essex, Fergus, Guelph, Hagersville, Hamilton, Hanover, Harriston, Hespeler, Jarvis, Kingston, Kingsville, Kitchener, Linwood, Listowel, London, Lucknow, Mono, Mount Forest, Neustadt, New Hamburg, Niagara-on-the-Lake, Oakville, Orangeville, Orillia, Owen Sound, Palmerston, Peterborough, Petrolia, Port Elgin, Preston, Rockwood, Sarnia, Seaforth, Sheffield, Shelburne, Simcoe, Southampton, St. Jacobs, St. Marys, St. Thomas, Stoney Creek, Stratford, Thamesford, Tillsonburg, Waterdown, Waterford, Waterloo, Welland, Wellesley, Windsor, Wingham, Woodstock

Book 114-116: Waterloo updated
Book 117-119: Windsor
Book 120-121: Amherstburg
Book 122: Essex
Book 123-124: Kingsville
Book 125-127: Woodstock
Book 128: Thamesford
Book 129-132: St. Marys
Book 133-136: Sarnia
Book 137: Petrolia
Book 138-139: Welland
Book 140-145: Kingston
Book 146-149: Ottawa
Book 150-151: Midland

Book 152: Penetanguishene
Book 153: Kemptville
Book 154: Cornwall
Book 155: Mariatown to Maitland
Book 156: Morrisburg

Other Books by Barbara Raue

Coins of Gold

Arrows, Indians and Love

The Life and Times of Barbara
Volume 1: Inventions That Have Enhanced My Life
Volume 2: Entertainment That I Have Enjoyed
Volume 3: East Coast Trips
Volume 4: Olympics Have Always Intrigued Me
Volume 5: Wonders of the World
Volume 6: Caribbean Cruises We Have Enjoyed
Volume 7: Animals
Volume 8: Storms and Other Major Disasters in My Lifetime
Volume 9: Wars, Terrorist Attacks and Major Disasters

The Cromwell Family Book

Laura Secord Discovered

Daddy Where Are You?

Montana Series
Book 1: Montana Dream
Book 2: Life on the Montana Frontier
Book 3: Montana to Boston and Back

Visit Barbara's website to view all of her books
http://barbararaue.ca

Table of Contents

Mariatown and Iroquois

South Dundas is a municipality in eastern Ontario in the United Counties of Stormont, Dundas and Glengarry along the north shore of the St. Lawrence River. It is located about sixty miles/one hundred kilometers south of Ottawa. The township was created on January 1, 1998, by amalgamating the former townships of Matilda and Williamsburg with the villages of Iroquois and Morrisburg. (Morrisburg is big enough to be a separate book.) Mariatown is located in the township.

The McIntosh apple was discovered and cultivated in South Dundas near Williamsburg. John McIntosh moved to Upper Canada in 1796. In 1811 he acquired a farm in Dundela, and while clearing the land of second growth discovered several apple seedlings. He transplanted these, and one bore the superior fruit which became famous as the McIntosh Red apple. John's son Allan established a nursery and promoted this new species extensively.

Morrisburg and Iroquois were partially flooded by the creation of the St. Lawrence Seaway in 1958. Unlike the Lost Villages of Cornwall and Osnabruck Townships, the two towns were relocated to higher ground in the same area.

An artificial lake, Lake Saint Lawrence, now extends from a hydroelectric dam at Cornwall to the control structure at Iroquois, and replaces the formerly narrow and turbulent section of river that was impassable to large vessels.

Cardinal

Edwardsburgh/Cardinal is a township in the United Counties of Leeds and Grenville of eastern Ontario. Edwardsburgh Township was surveyed in 1783. The Township of Edwardsburgh/Cardinal was formed on January 1, 2001, through the amalgamation of Edwardsburgh Township with the Village of Cardinal. It is a historical community with many old homes and buildings, including one-room school houses, grist mills, and churches. It is situated along the St. Lawrence River and extends back into rural hamlets. The South Nation River passes through the township. The township's main population centres are Cardinal, Johnstown, and Spencerville.

Ten percent of the area's water drains into the St. Lawrence, while ninety percent drains into the South Nation River. The flow of the South Nation River through this area is very sluggish with poor drainage, due to the fact there is little drop in elevation along the river; this leads to the formation of bogs and swamps, and also makes the area prone to seasonal flooding.

Up until the 18th century, the land was covered with thick, mature, mixed forests. The original forest was almost completely cleared throughout the years and the forest that stands today is mostly secondary growth over previously cleared land. The forests in the area presently contain numerous types of deciduous oak, birch, ash and maple trees. The common coniferous trees in the area include many types of pine and cedar as well as balsam fir and white spruce. In the darker, acidic soils around the bogs and swamps there are tamarack trees, as well as juniper and black spruce.

In 1673, the French, working with native tribes from the area, built a storehouse on Old Breeches River, now known as Johnstown Creek. This storehouse was used to hold supplies for upriver trading posts such as Fort Frontenac (now Kingston). In 1759, The French settlers built Fort de Levis on Chimney Island, in the St. Lawrence River just off of Johnstown, between it and Ogdensburg. The purpose of this fort was to protect the St. Lawrence River from the British. It was captured by Major-General Jeffrey Amherst in August 1760 during the Battle of the Thousand Islands. The island on which the fort once stood was permanently flooded during the construction of the St. Lawrence Seaway.

Johnstown

Before the construction of dams and later the Seaway, Johnstown was fronted by a calm section of the St. Lawrence River located between two rapids. By 1784, Loyalists were residing in the township and until 1790 the landing point and base camp for these settlers was at Johnstown.

Johnstown is part of the township of Edwardsburgh/Cardinal in the United Counties of Leeds and Grenville in eastern Ontario. It is located at the Canadian terminus of the Ogdensburg-Prescott International Bridge.

In 1792 John Graves Simcoe, the first Lieutenant Governor of Upper Canada, established himself in Johnstown which then became the district's administrative seat. This led to the court of quarter sessions (the district's government) alternating its meeting location between Johnstown and Cornwall, and to the construction of a courthouse and gaol. The courthouse was a log structure, which stood near the present site of the Prescott-Ogdensburg Bridge. By the late 1790s, the village was also home to a sawmill, gristmill, and an inn and tavern. Census records indicate by 1807, there were thirty-six houses and a general store. In 1808, the Seat of Justice was moved to Elizabethtown (now Brockville), as it was a more central location in the district.

New Wexford is located in Edwardsburgh/Cardinal Township, in the United Counties of Leeds and Grenville of eastern Ontario.

Prescott

Prescott is a small town located on the north shore of the Saint Lawrence River in the United Counties of Leeds and Grenville. Colonel Edward Jessup remained loyal to the British during the revolutionary war. He was granted 1,000 acres and in 1810 had building lots surveyed for the town which he named in honor of General Robert Prescott who had been Governor-in-Chief of Canada between 1797 and 1807.

Prescott was a strategic military site for the protection of the Canadian border against American and French invasions. Fort Wellington was built in 1812 to defend the St. Lawrence River and the town. Prescott is located at the head of the St. Lawrence rapids. Before the completion of the canals between here and Montreal in 1847, Prescott was the eastern terminus of Great Lakes navigation.

Established in 1810, it became a center for the forwarding, or shipping, trade and an important center in Montreal's commercial system. One of the earliest forwarders at Prescott was Captain William Gilkison who began operations in 1811. The population of Upper Canada increased rapidly after 1820; the trade expanded and forwarding firms, including Henderson & Hooker, and Macpherson, Crane & Co., established ship building yards, wharves, and warehouses along the waterfront. The forwarding trade flourished before the building of railways and canals. The railway came in 1854.

During four days in November 1838, British troops and local militia defeated an invasion force of 300 American hunters and Canadian rebels. The Battle of the Windmill victory prevented the invasion force from capturing Fort Wellington in Prescott and cutting the St. Lawrence communications link, which would have left Upper Canada open to invasion.

By 1887, in addition to the fort, barracks, and military hospital, there were twenty-three hotels, twenty-four taverns, a distillery, two breweries, two foundries, two tanneries, two potters, a bank, a saw mill, a quarry, a brick factory, a shipyard, a grain elevator, and a farmers' market building.

With a town of 3,000 people, smaller establishments and services were also present: a bowling alley, a theatre, several newspapers, a telegraph office, bakeries, general merchants, doctors' offices, a dentist, a library, a college, two schools, four churches, many docks and wharves with large storage buildings, and a ferry service to Ogdensburg, New York.

Maitland

Maitland is a small village in the United Counties of Leeds and Grenville. It is located along the St. Lawrence River about five kilometers east of the City of Brockville. Loyalists began to settle the area in the late 1700s and into the early 19th century by building homesteads, establishing businesses and opening small factories. During the early part of the century, Maitland was on the opposite end of a supply route running to Merrick's Mills, which aided in its growth; the construction of the Welland Canal and other canal systems through the St. Lawrence allowed goods to be transported to and from the village. A wharf was used for collecting goods, and many mills were constructed.

One of Maitland's most notable landmarks was constructed in 1828: the Longley Tower, which was originally built as a windmill along the St. Lawrence River. The tower had a brief life as a windmill, but it did not generate enough power to sustain anything for long; it was later converted into a distillery. Longley imported a steam engine from Europe, built a flour mill, and constructed a stone building out of which he ran a general store and post office. Major Charles Lemon constructed two mills, a foundry, and a blacksmith shop to serve the village.

Mariatown

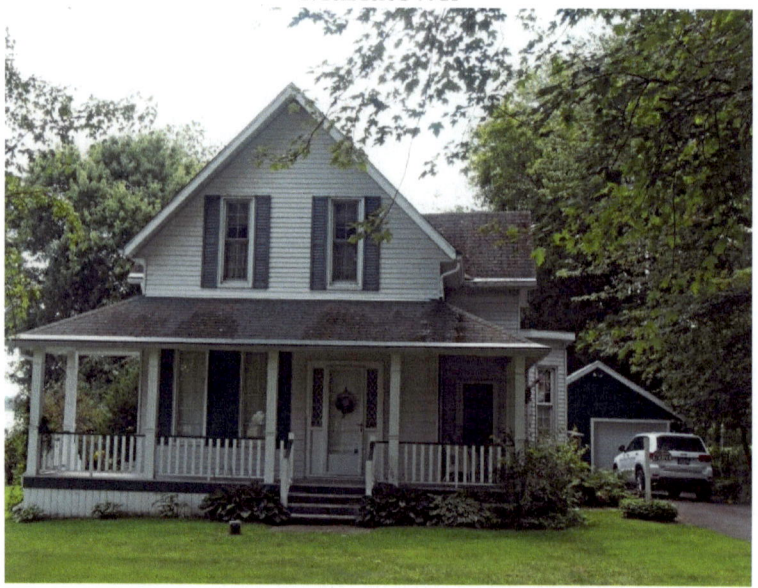

Square pillars supporting verandah with open railing; sidelights

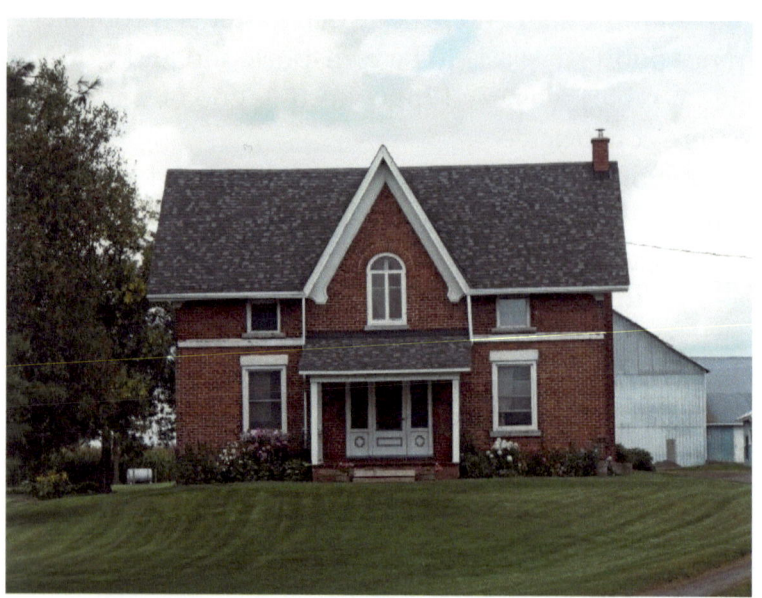

Gothic – semi-circular window in gable

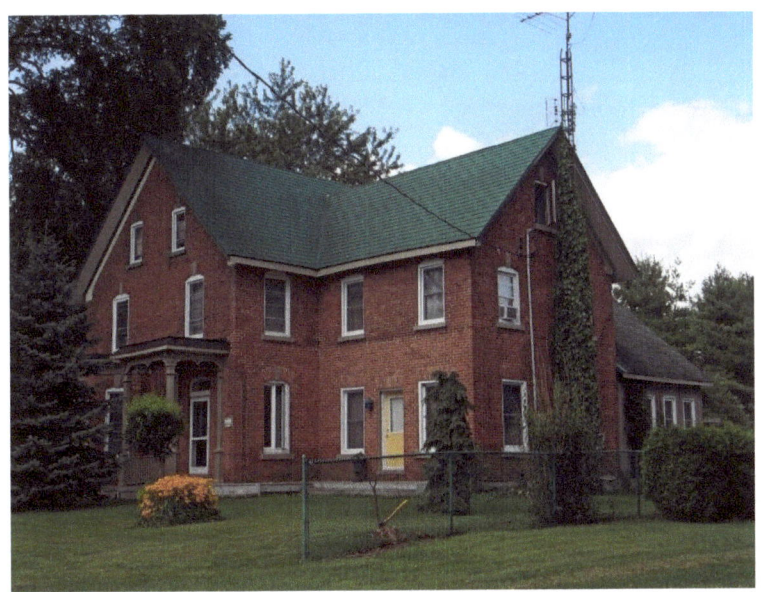

Gothic – gable roof, voussoirs with keystones

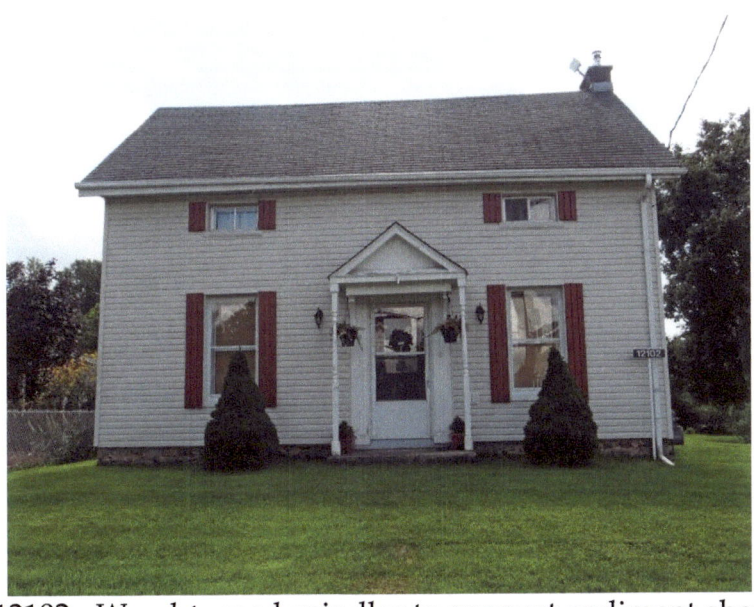

#12102 - Wood-turned spindles to support pediment above door

Mariatown

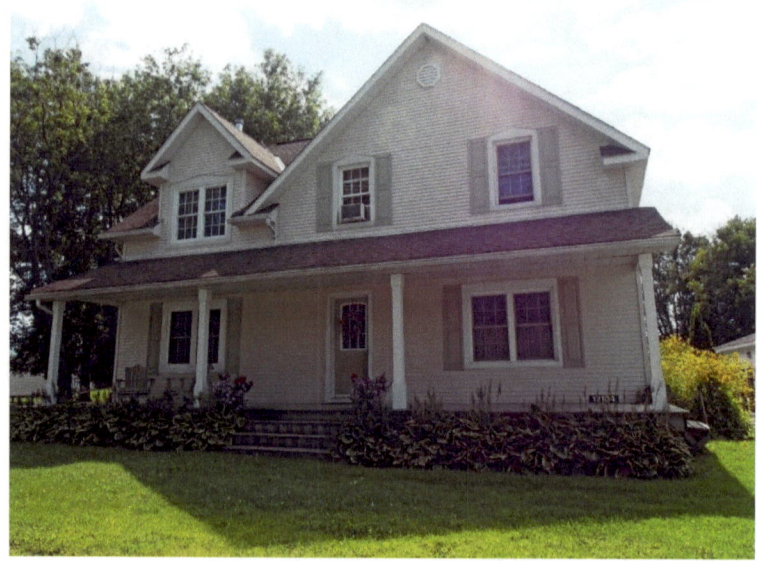

Cornice return on gables

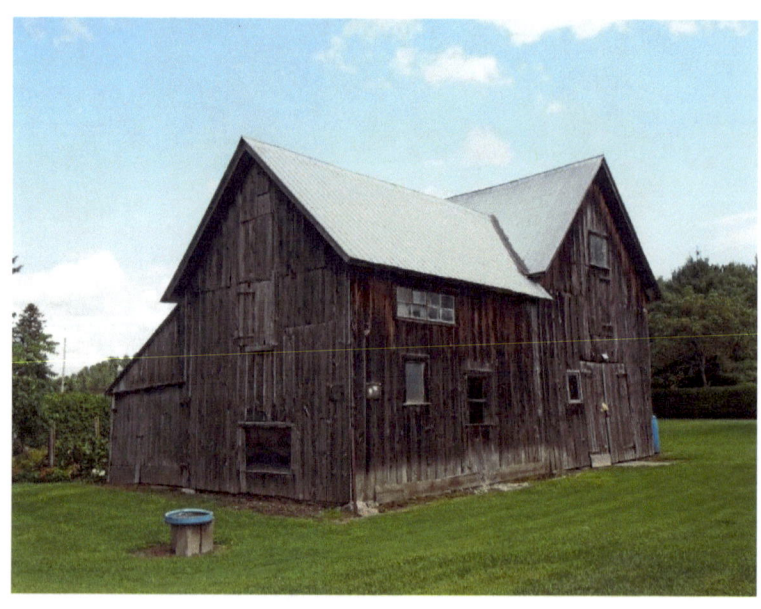

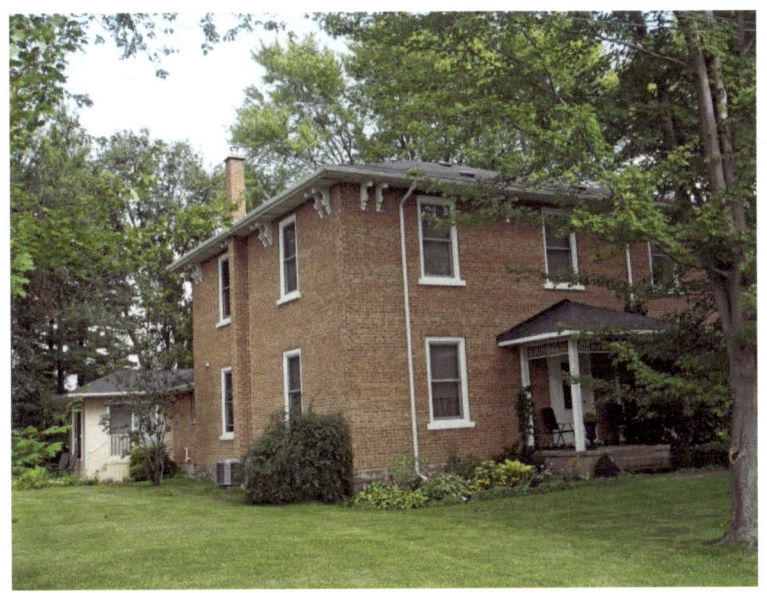

Hipped roof, paired cornice brackets

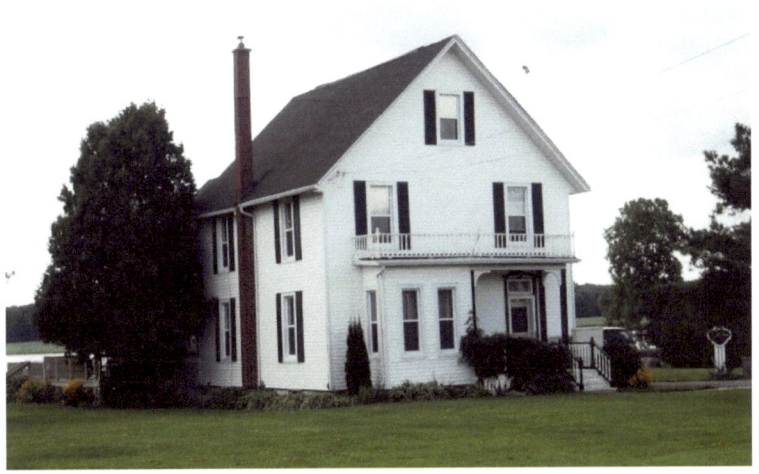

2½ storeys, second floor balcony with open railing above rectangular bay window and open porch

Mariatown

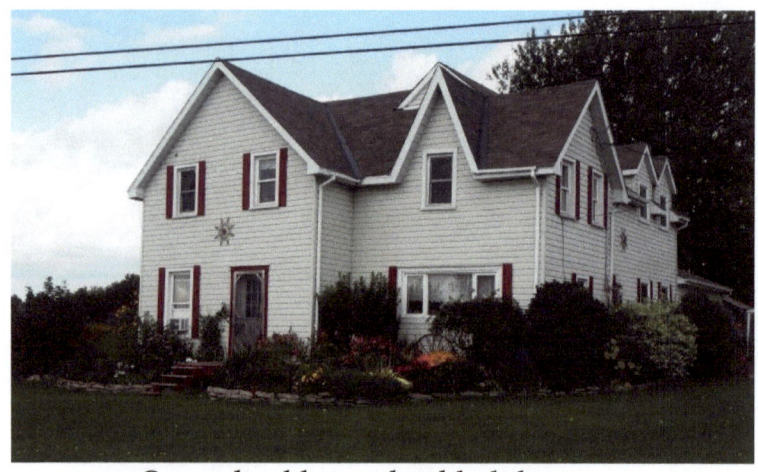

Several gables and gabled dormers

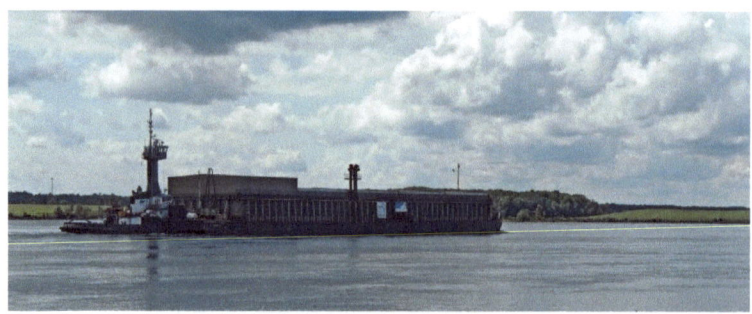

Ship on the water

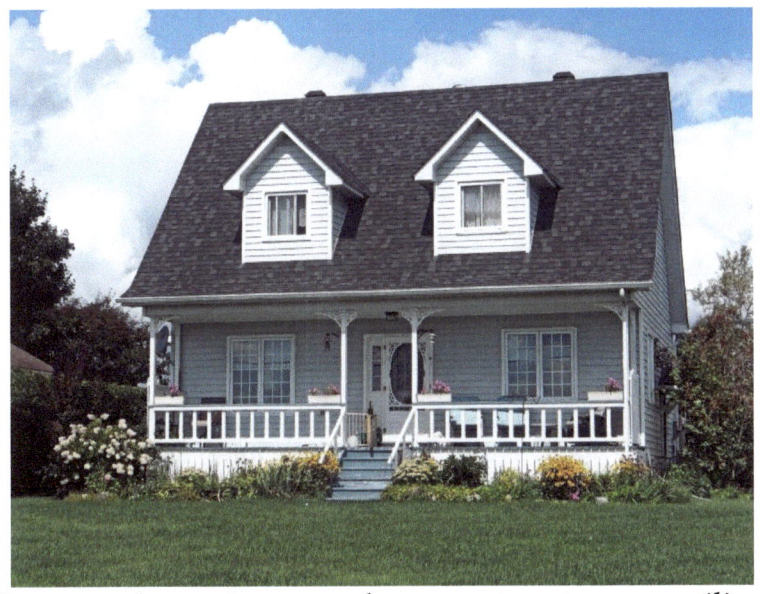

Dormers, decorative veranda support posts, open railing; sidelights

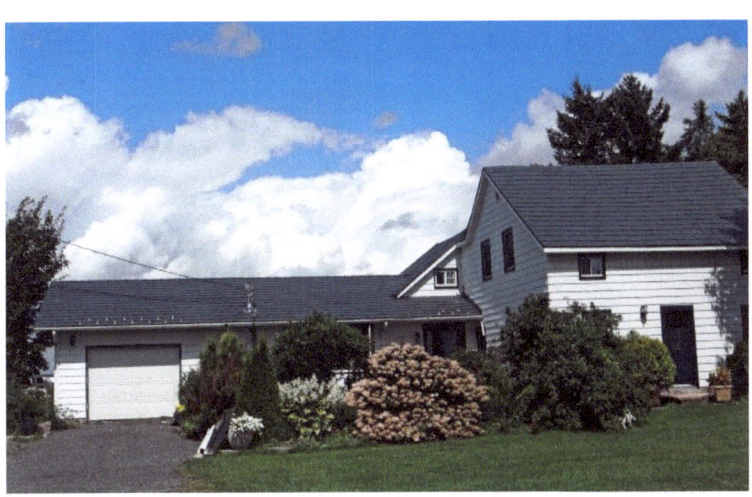

Mariatown

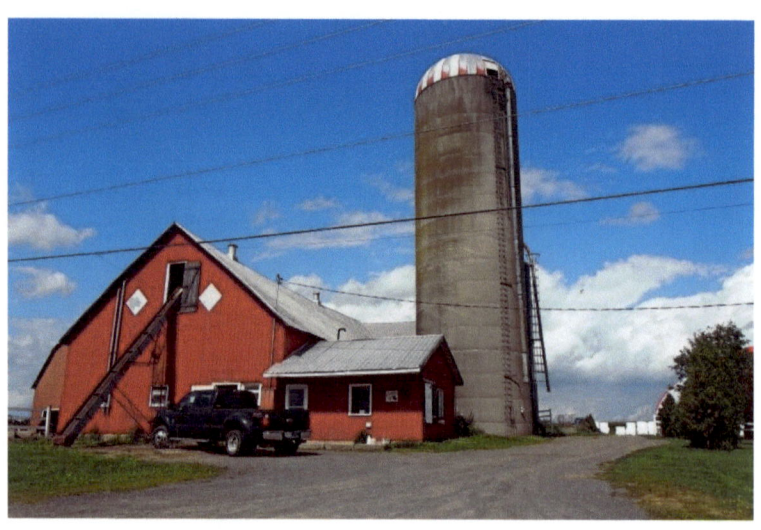

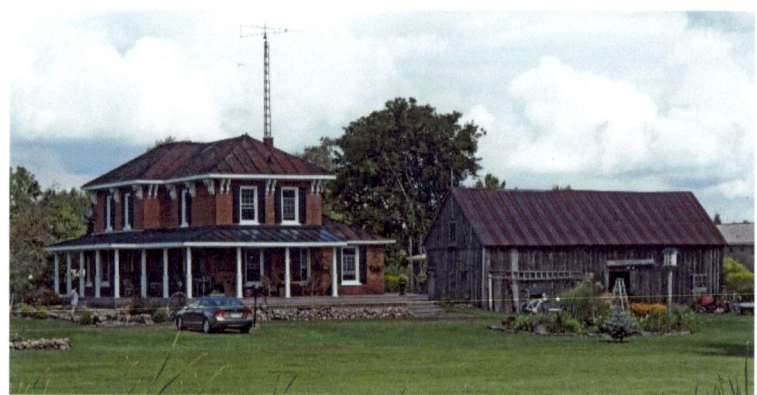

Steeply-pitched hipped roof, cornice brackets, open
wraparound verandah

Iroquois

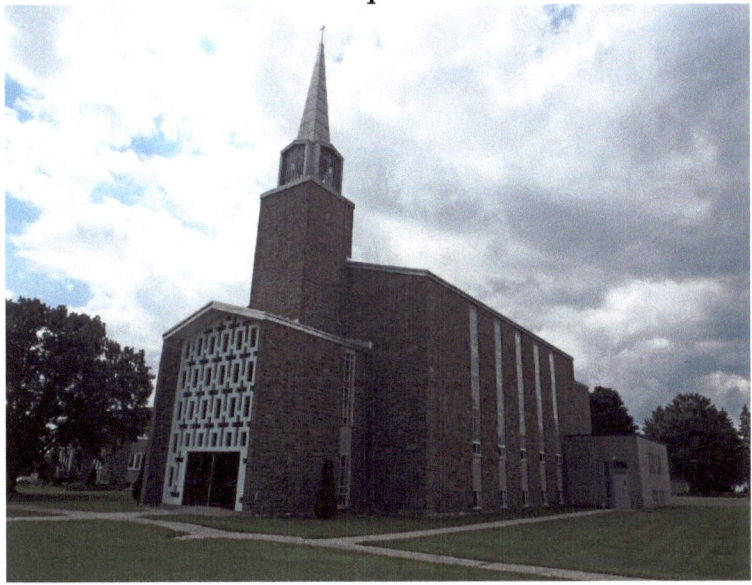

Iroquois United Church

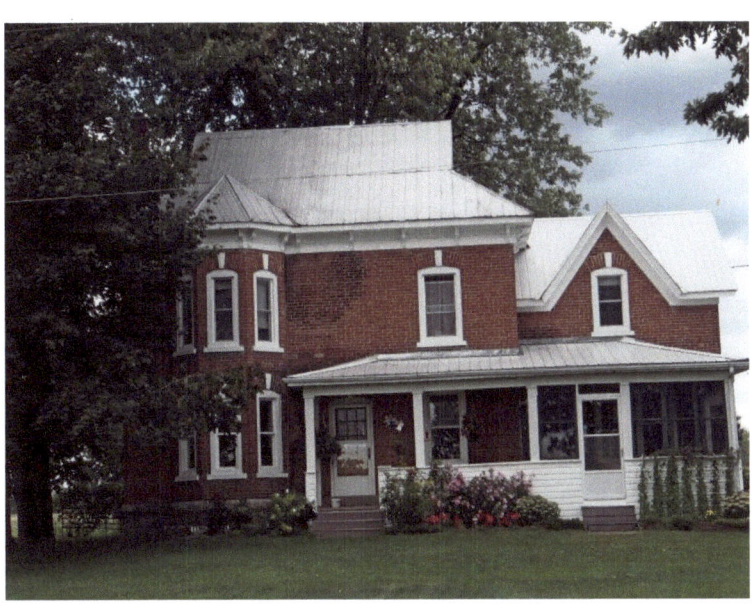

Two-storey bay window; voussoirs with keystones; cornice brackets

Iroquois

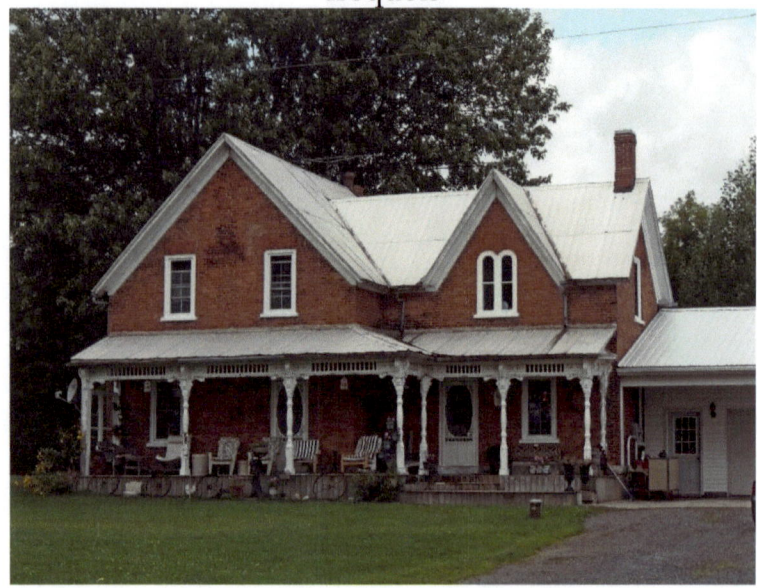

Victorian - decorative veranda support posts, no railing

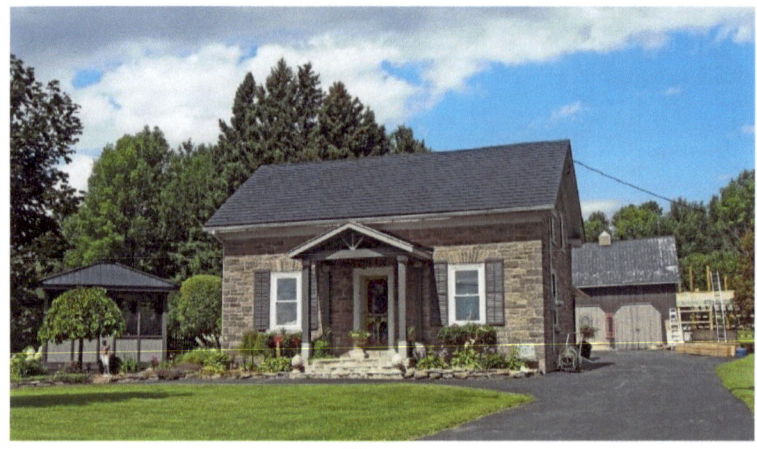

Stone

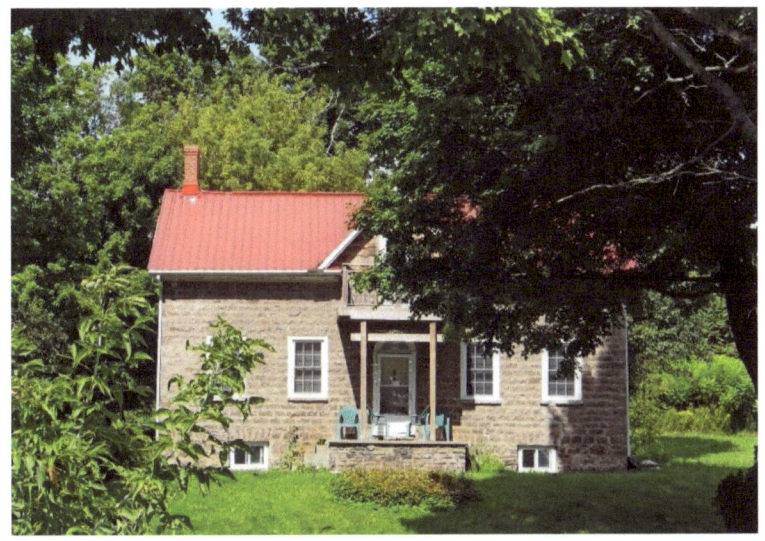

Stone, second floor balcony

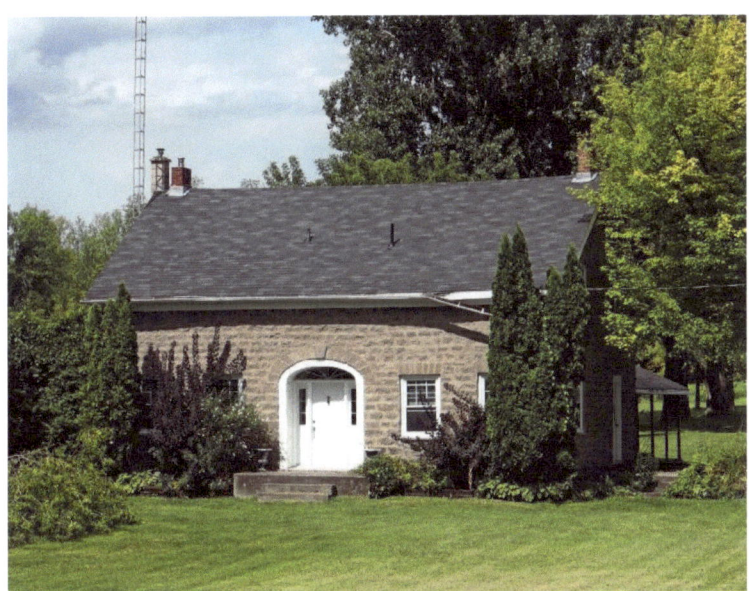

Stone, voussoirs with keystones, sidelights and transom

Cardinal

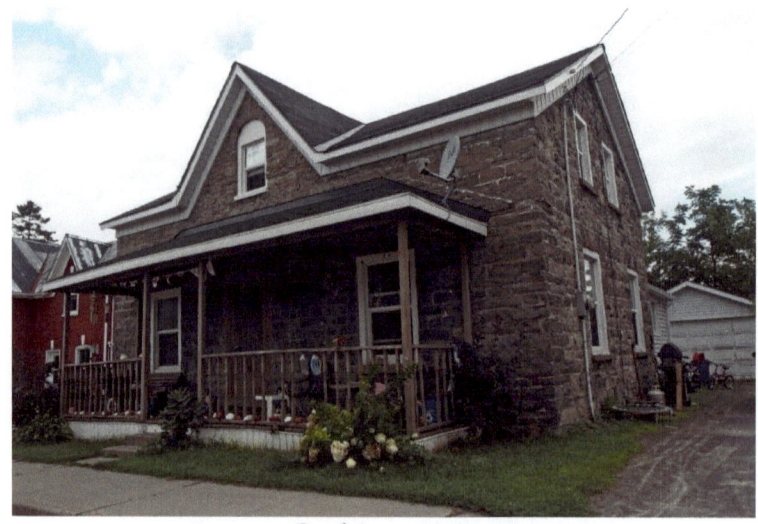

Gothic - stone

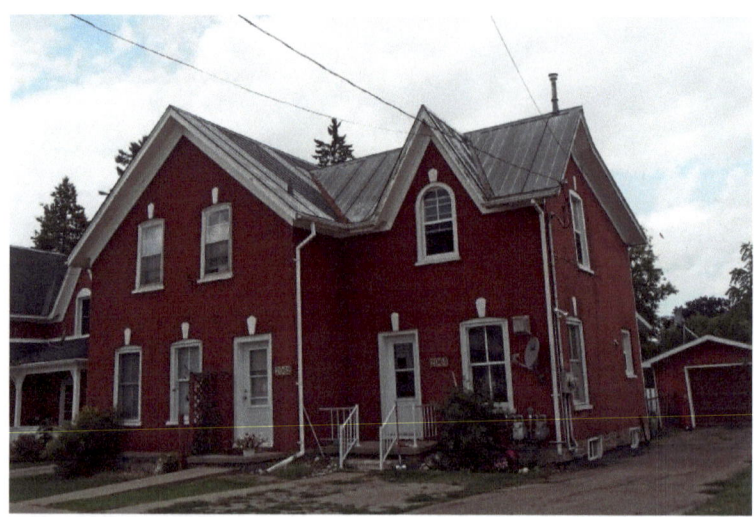

2062-2064 - Victorian style – voussoirs with keystones

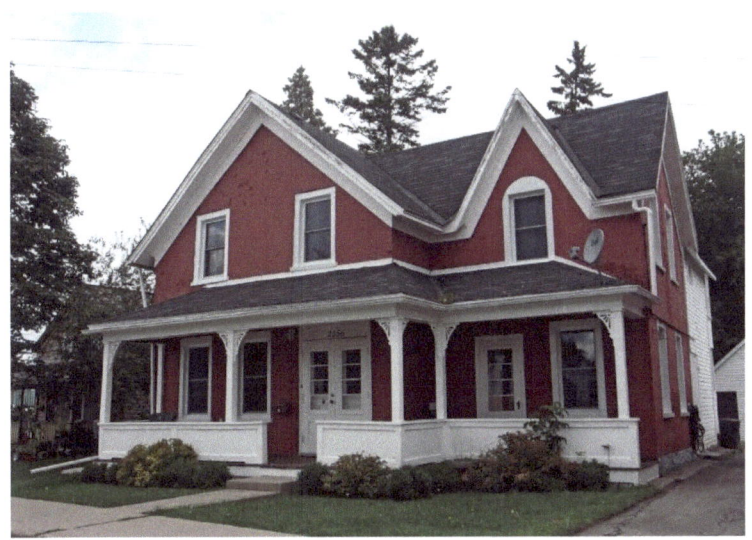

2056 - Victorian style

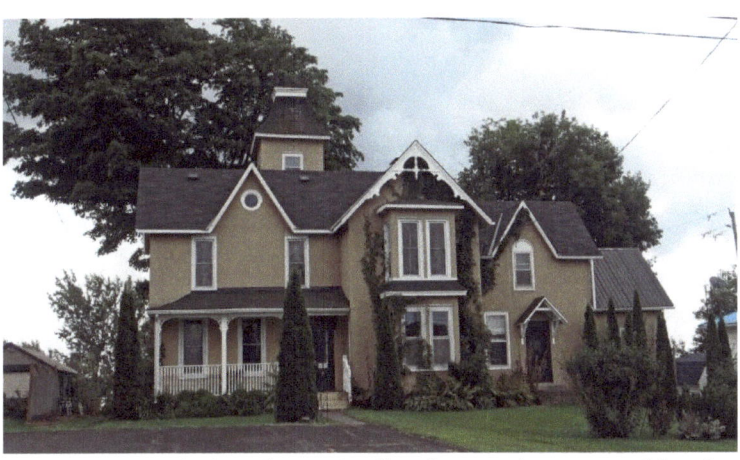

Victorian – semi-circular spindle decoration on gable above two-storey rectangular bay windows; three-storey tower with iron cresting on top; decorative veranda support posts, open railing

Cardinal

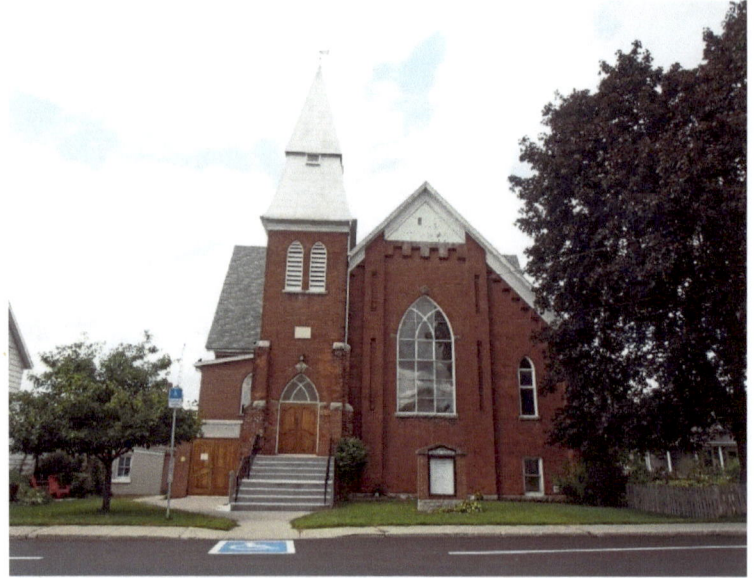

2120 - St. John's United Church, Cardinal – 1888 – Gothic Revival style – lancet windows, buttresses

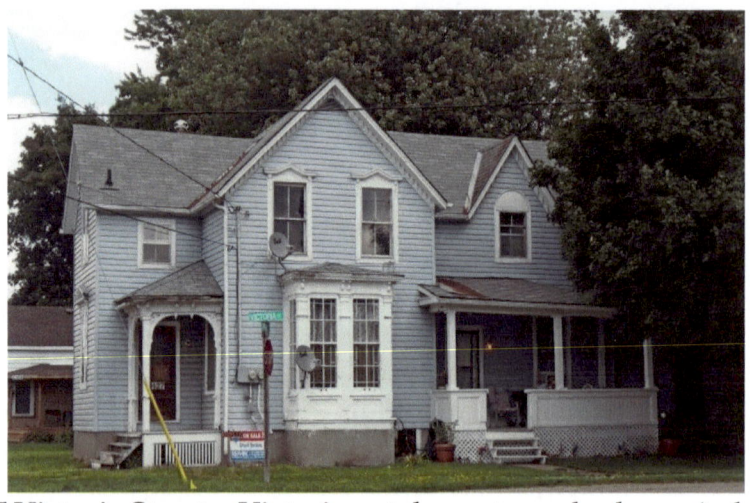

427 Victoria Street – Victorian style, rectangular bay window, decorative veranda support posts

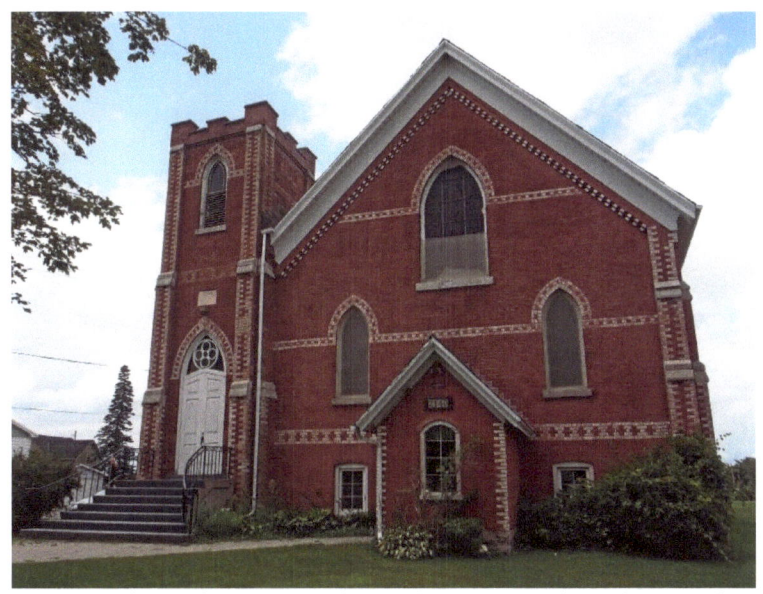

St. Andrew's and St. James' Presbyterian Church, Cardinal –
A.D. 1877 – Gothic - dichromatic brickwork, dentil moulding,
banding, corner quoins

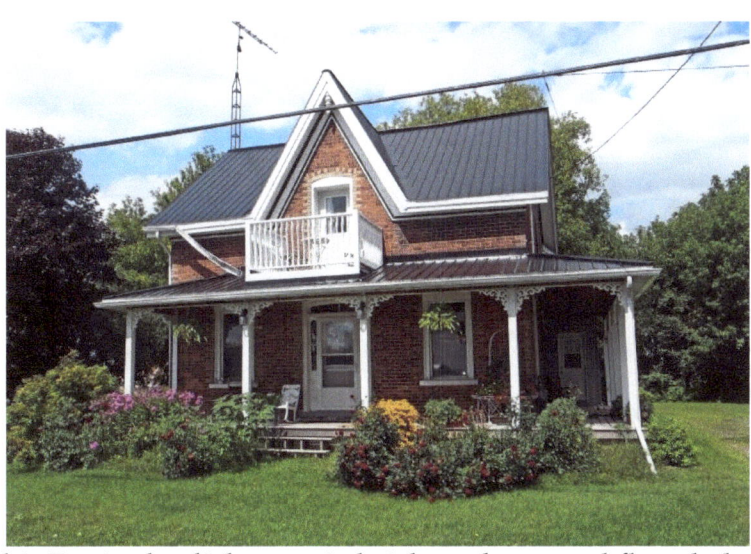

Gothic Revival – dichromatic brickwork, second floor balcony,
decorative veranda support posts; sidelight, transom

Cardinal

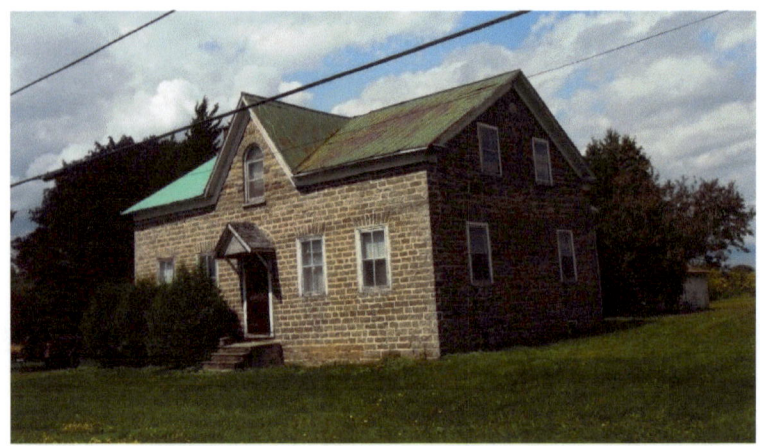

Gothic – semi-circular window in front gable; voussoirs

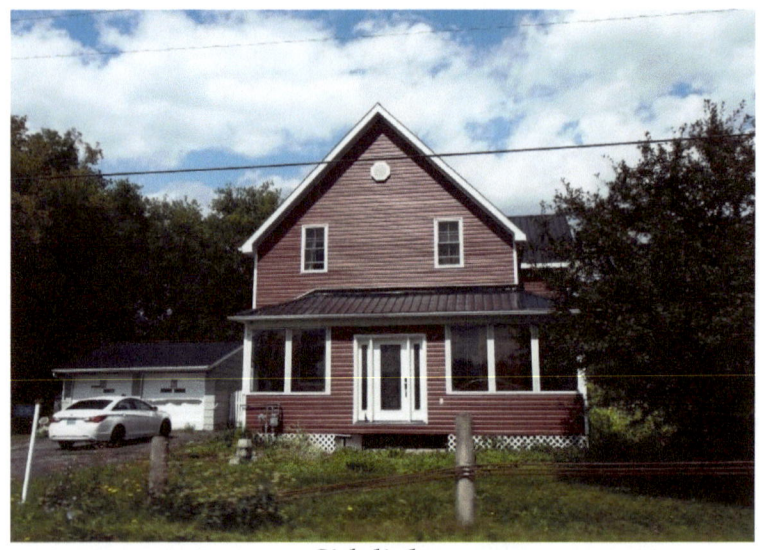

Sidelights

Cardinal

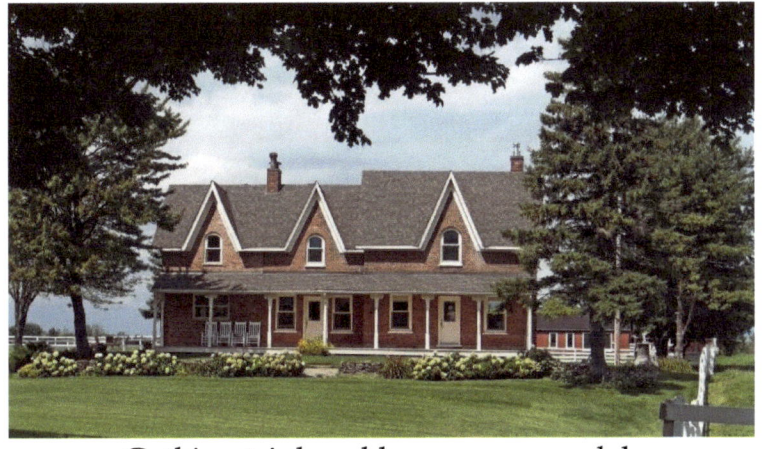

Gothic – triple gables, open verandah

Johnstown

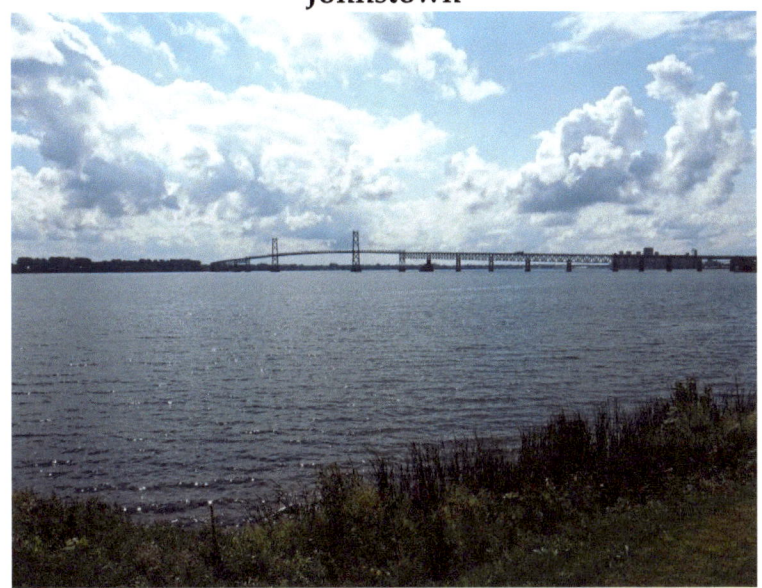

Prescott-Ogdensburg Bridge

Johnstown

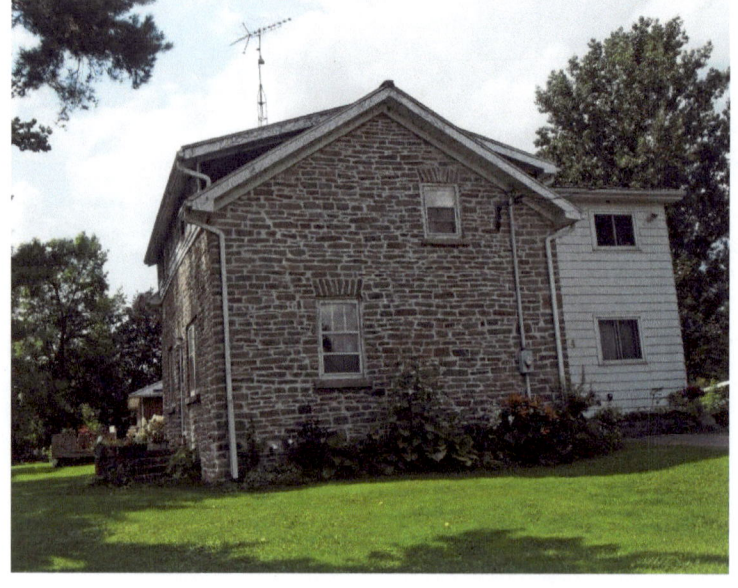

Cobblestone, shed dormer, voussoirs

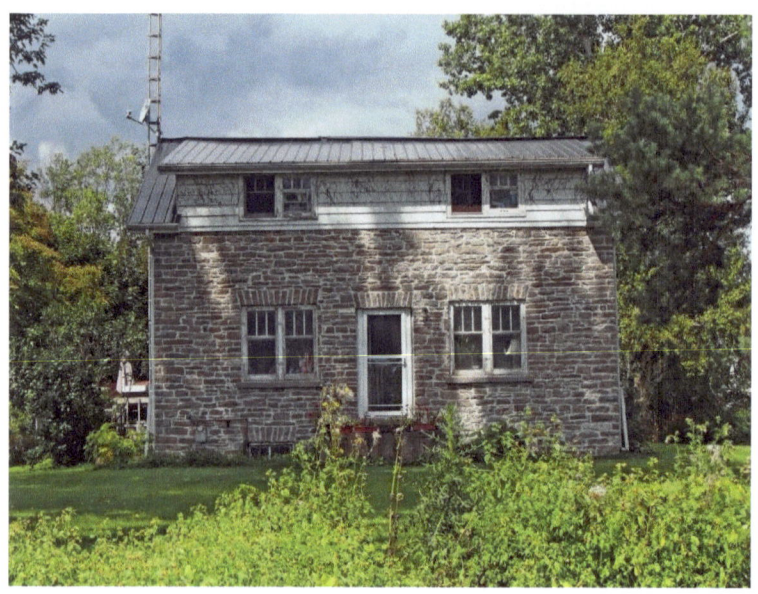

New Wexford

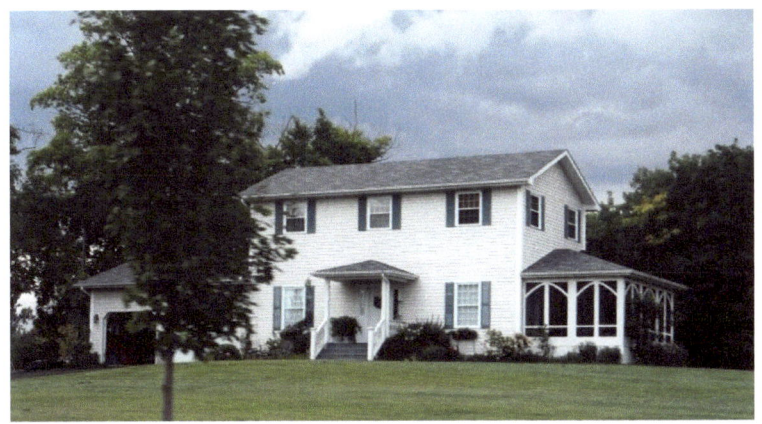

Georgian style

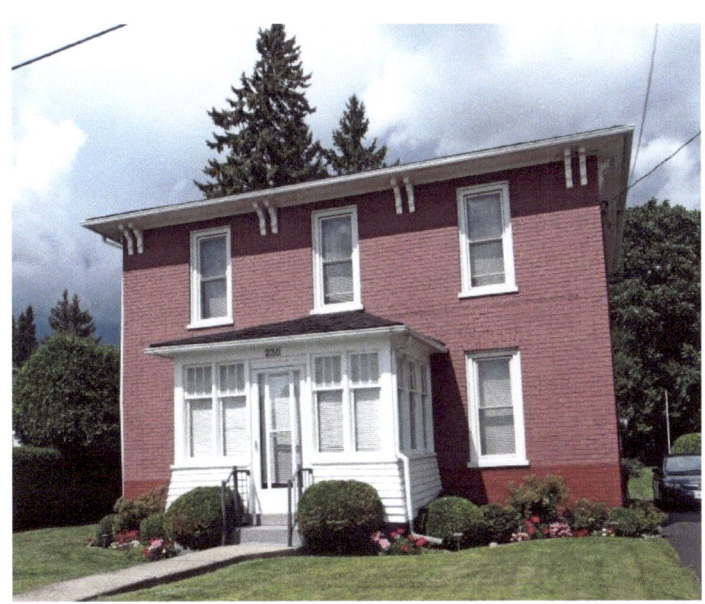

Hipped roof, paired cornice brackets, enclosed porch

Prescott

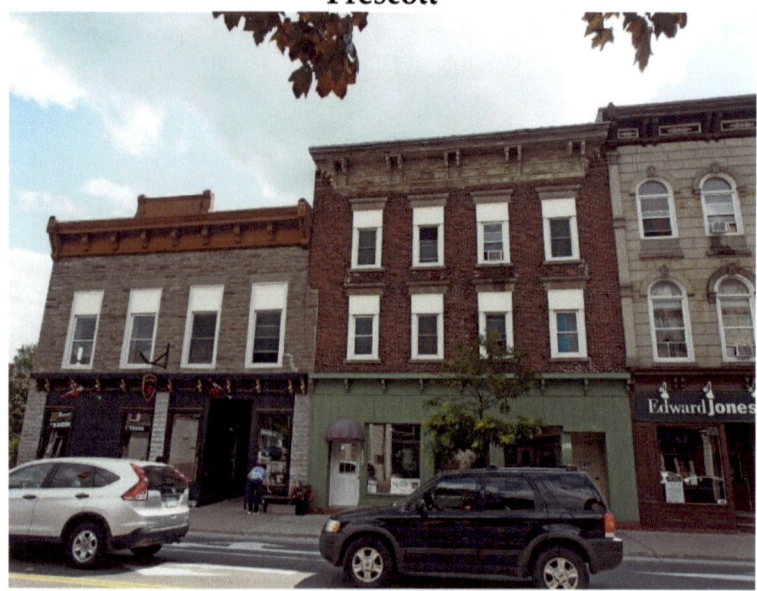

Italianate architectural style – 1874 - cornice brackets, window hoods

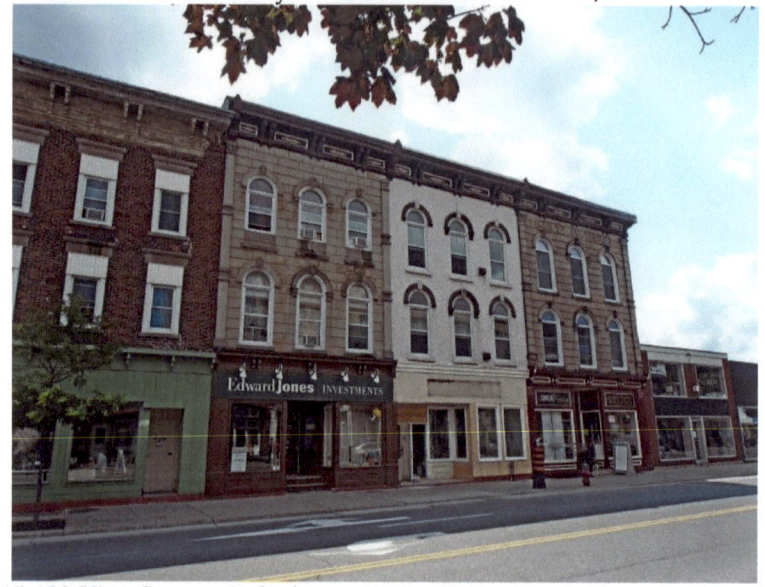

115-123 King Street - Italianate – 1874 – Keilty Block (Stern Building) -
stone-on-brick façade, limestone round-headed windows, flat roof,
decorative cornice, pilasters, keystones - facade uses different building
materials to divide the block into three equal sections

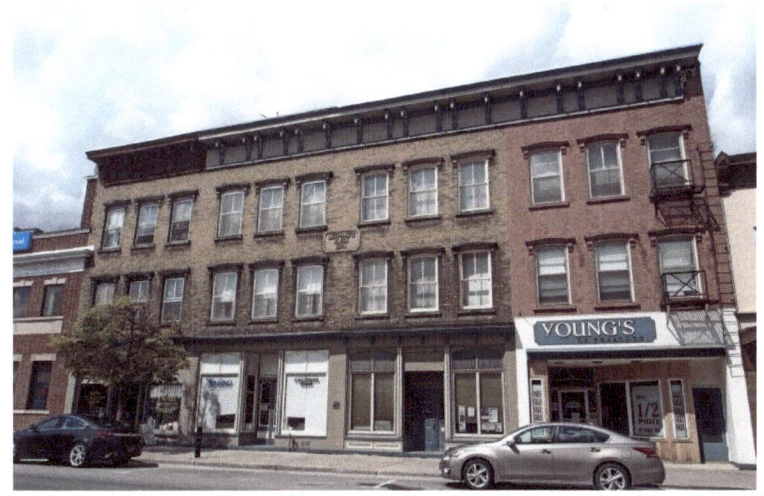

Mechanics Block – 1874 – cornice brackets, window hoods

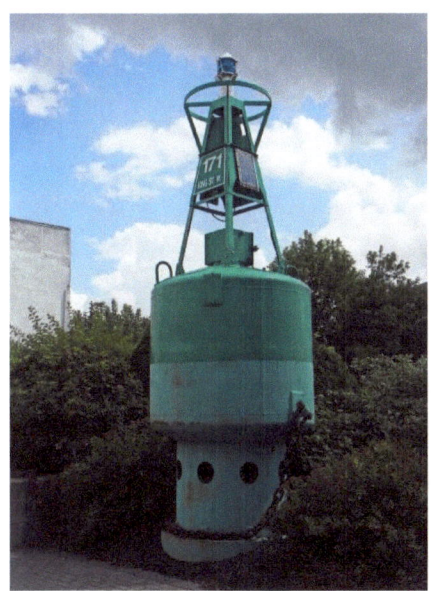

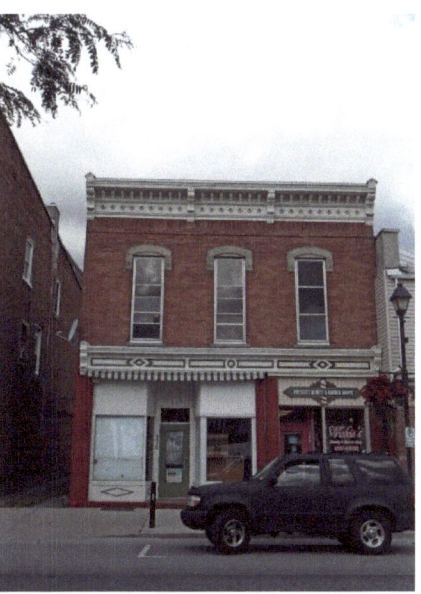

Typical 6 foot diameter lake and
river solar-powered light buoy

decorative cornice,
brackets

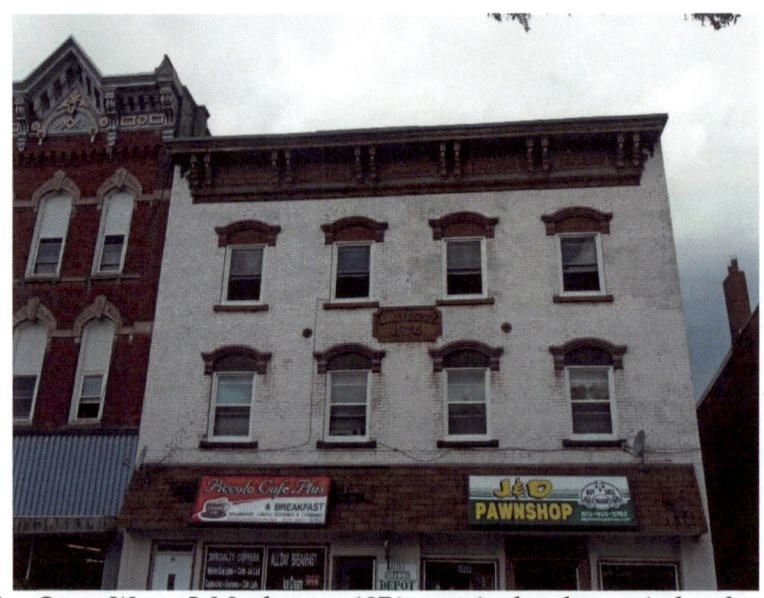

King Street West - J. Mayberry – 1874 - cornice brackets, window hoods

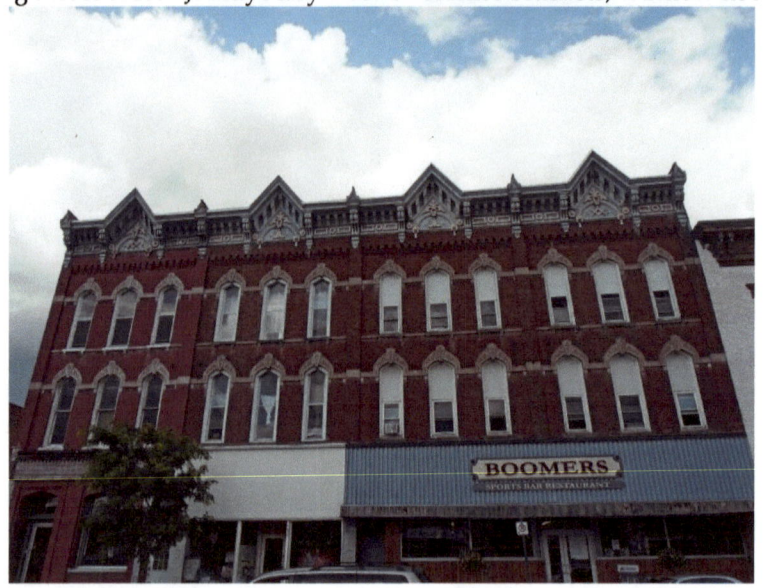

186-198 King Street West – Masonic Block – 1879 - building is composed of four sections three storeys high; arched windows with cornices and keystones decorated with linear designs; cornice brackets, bevelled dentil moulding; over the central bay of each section is a symbol of the Masonic Order

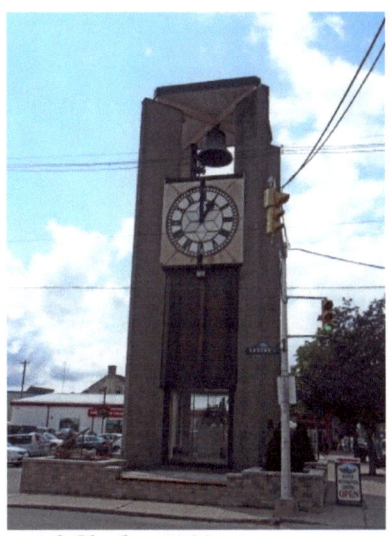

L. H. Daniels Memorial Clock – 1980 – in memory of Louis Hasbrouck Daniels, presented by his widow Harriet Daniels

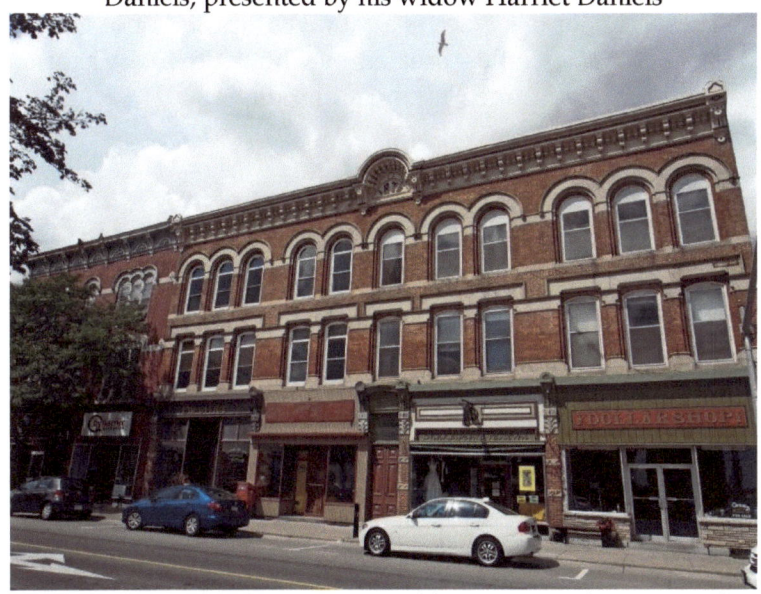

202-214 King Street West – Davis Building - 1878 – three-storey brick building with matching bays of windows starting with the Centre window with an arched, decorative cornice in limestone with etchings; next bay has two windows and the last outside bays have three windows with decorative cornices; across the top is a bracketed cornice running the full length of the roof, with an arch highlighting the center of the building.

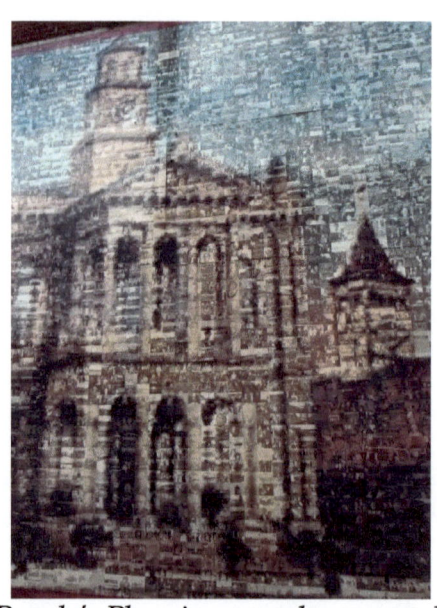

The Prescott People's Place is a mural composed of over 3,000 pictures of Prescott people – created by Chuck Street – Victoria Hall and St. John's Market

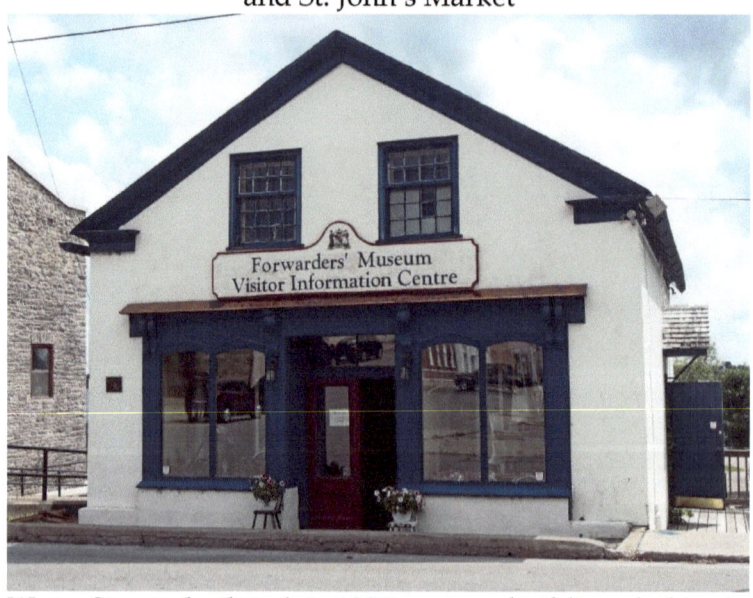

201 Water Street - built in late 1820s – stone building clad in stucco; first served as a post office and custom's house; cornice return on gable

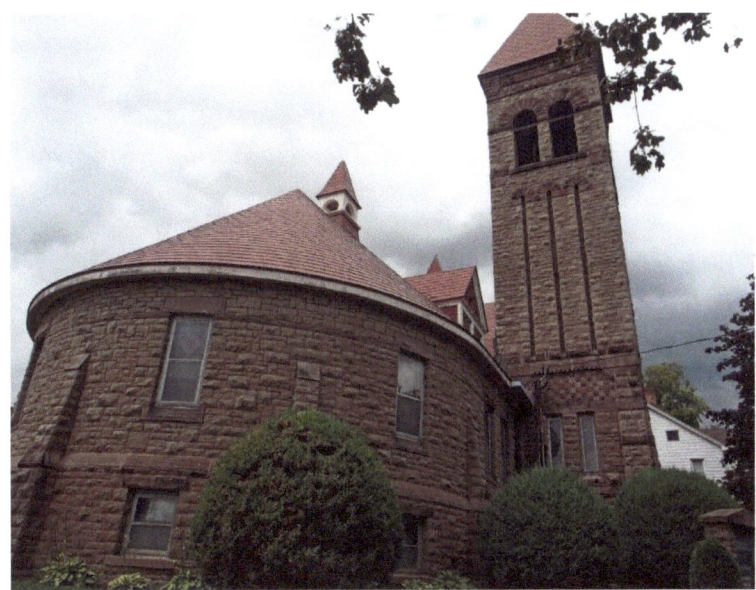

461 Centre Street - St. Andrew's Presbyterian Church – Romanesque style

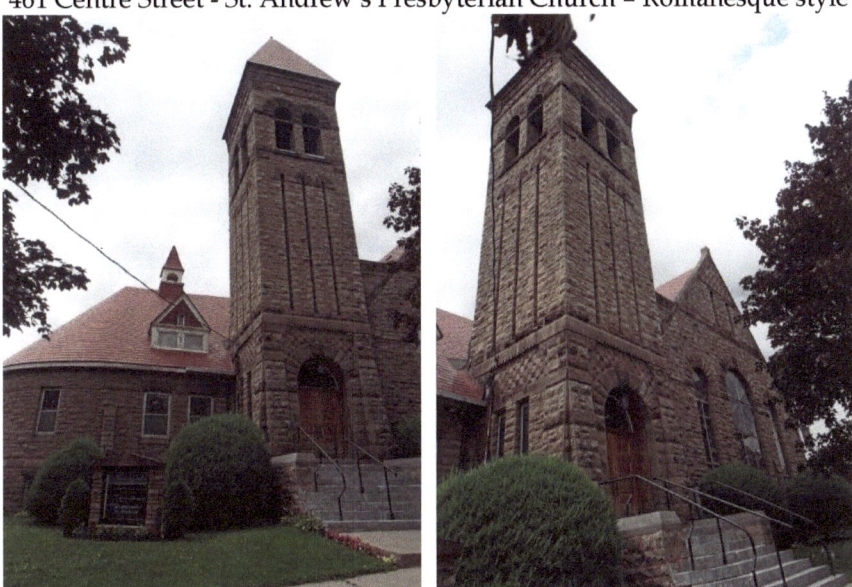

Harry Horwood came to Canada from England in the early 1850s and started work as a stained glass maker in Toronto. In 1881 he established his own business in Prescott and Horwood's stained glass windows can be found in Blue Church, St. John's Anglican, and St. Andrews churches.

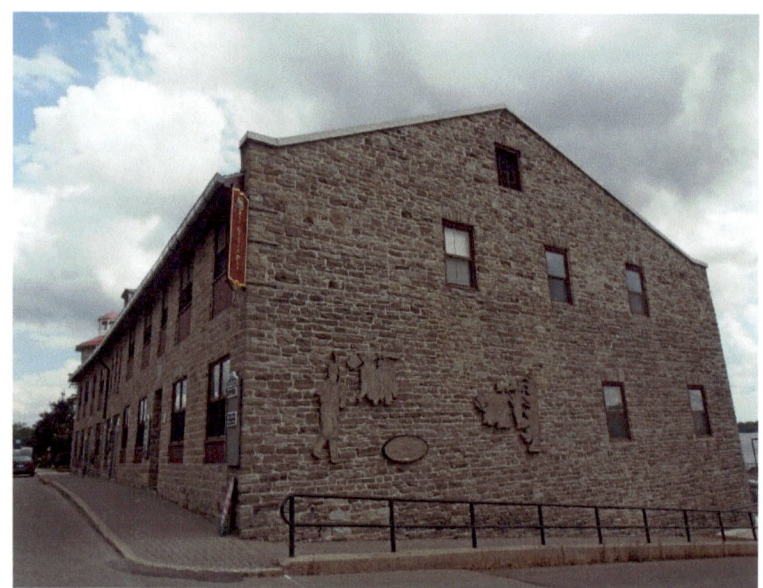

Stone building - Prescott raid on Ogdensburg plaque

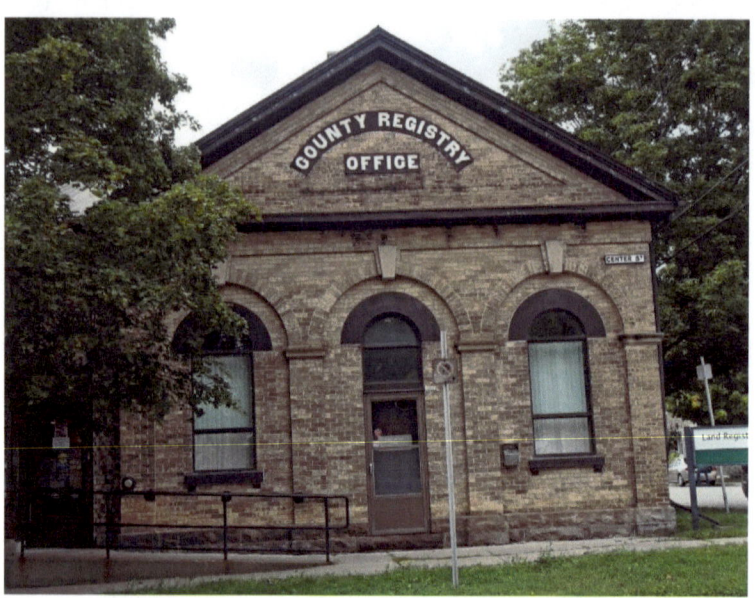

Centre Street - voussoirs with keystones

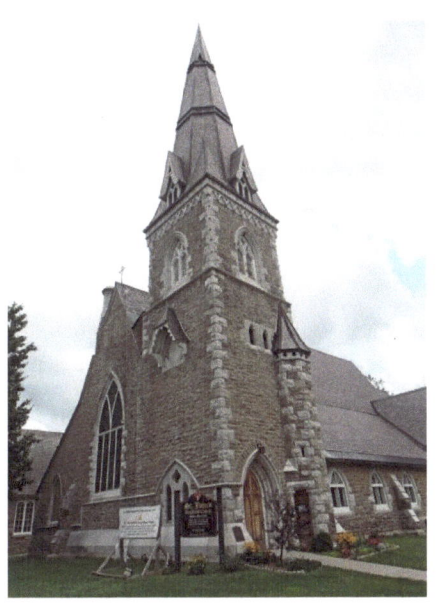

490 Centre Street - St. John the Evangelist Anglican Church –
Gothic – 1860 – stone building, lancet windows, buttresses,
corner quoins

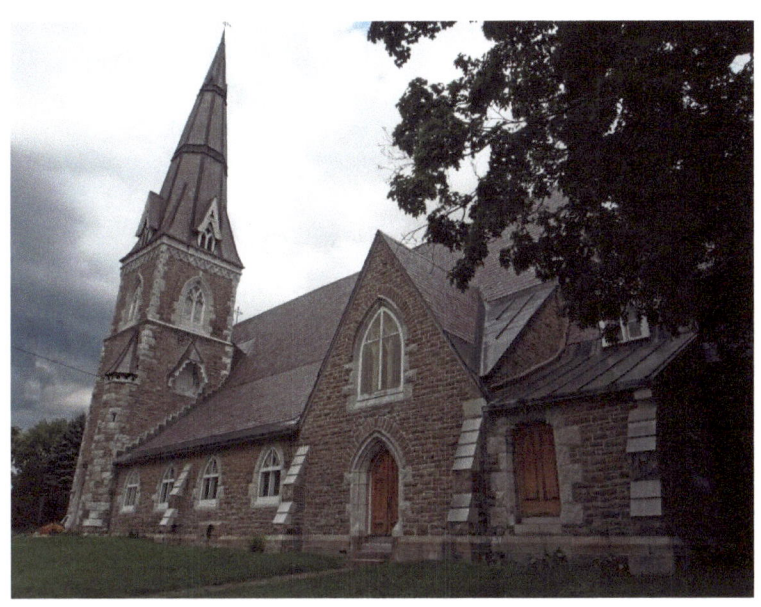

Prescott

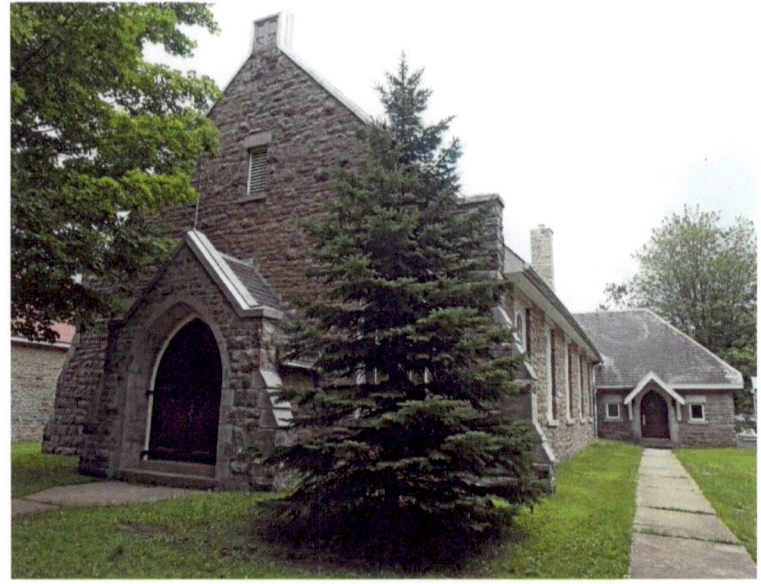

St. John's Memorial Hall, Prescott

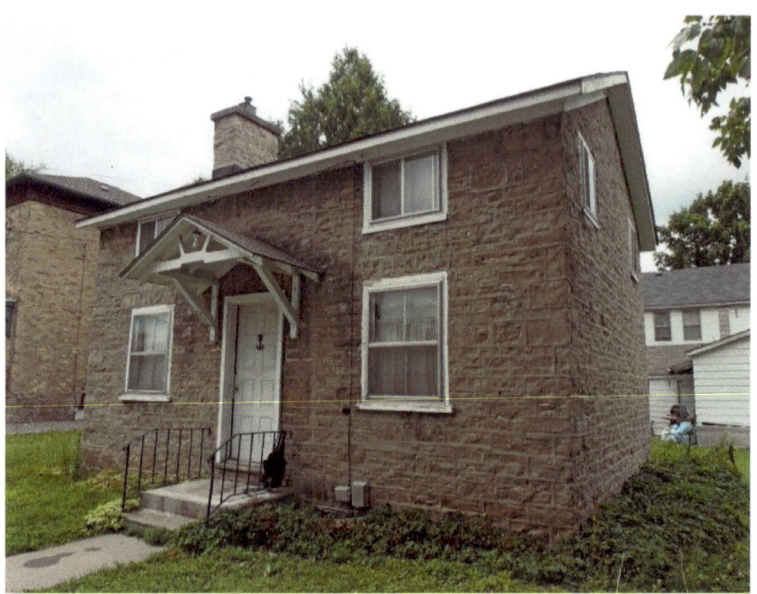

Stone

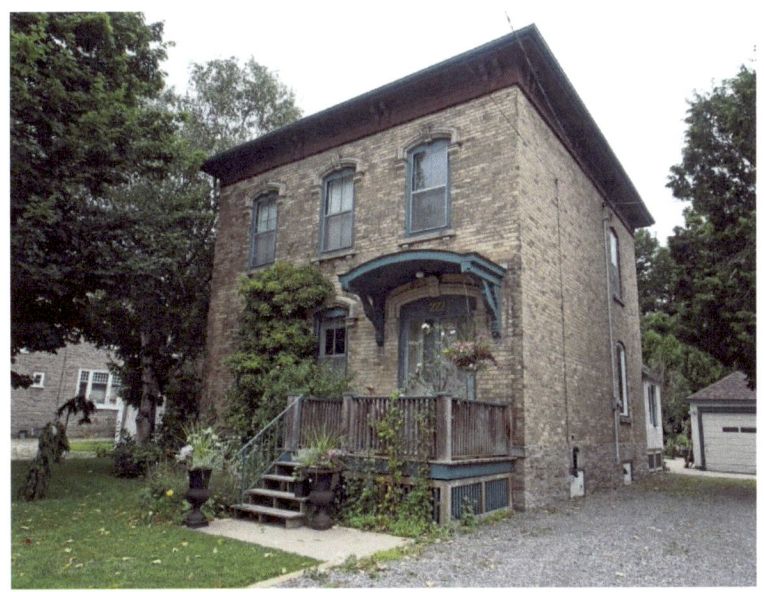

222 George Street – stone – hipped roof, paired cornice
brackets, drip moulds with keystones

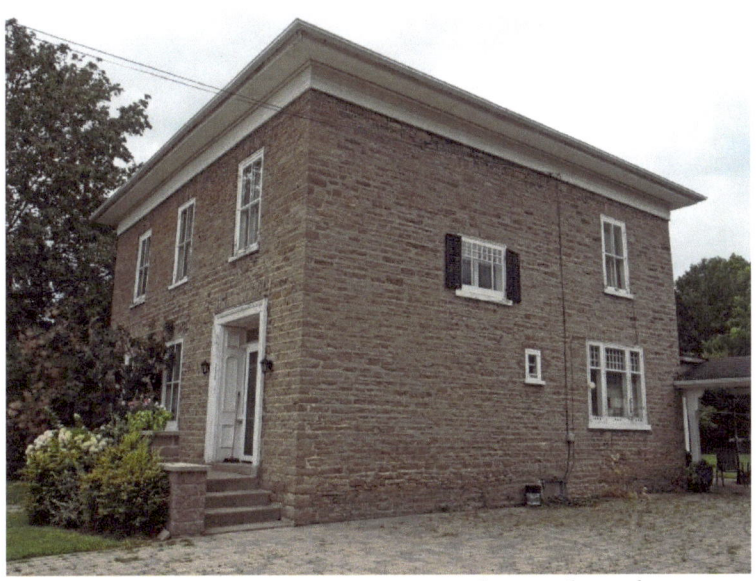

238 George Street – stone, hipped roof

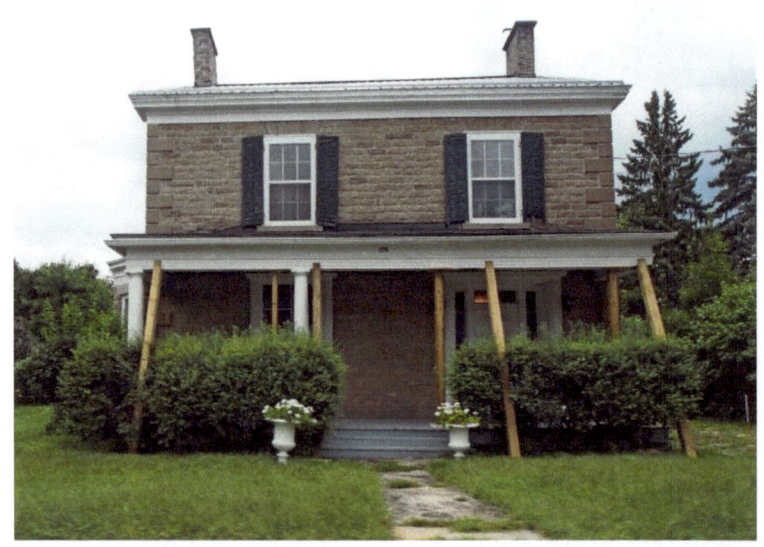

256 George Street – stone, hipped roof, columns with Doric capitals supporting veranda roof

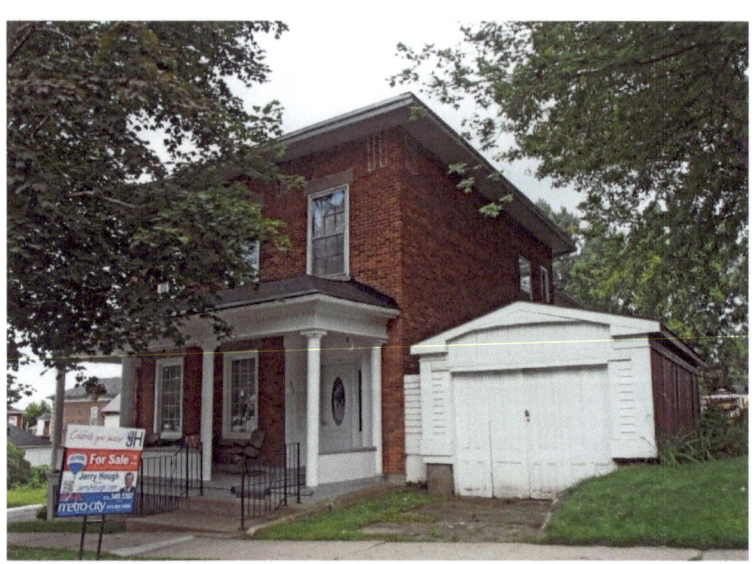

363 George Street – brick, hipped roof, columns with Doric capitals supporting veranda roof

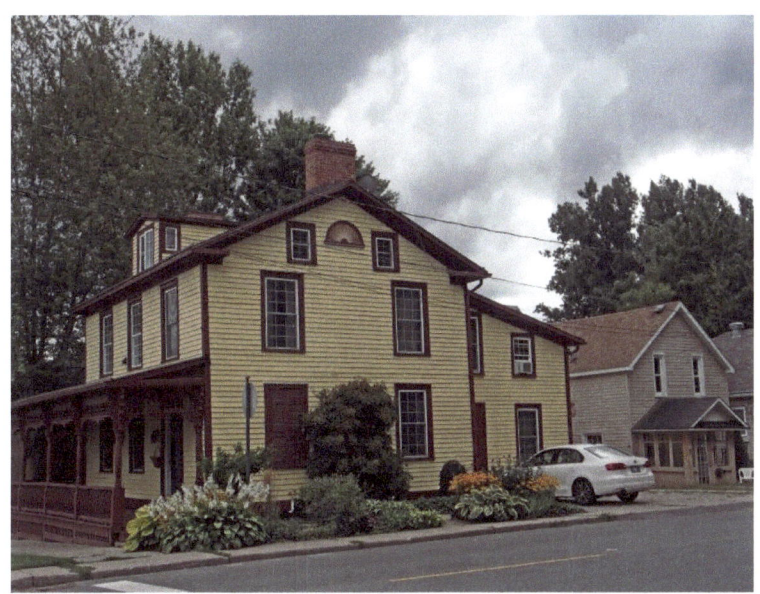

393 George Street - Frederick Belfoy House – 1840s - Georgian style with some unique features – instead of a center hall, it has the door on the right and a side hall; wooden frame and clapboard siding; cornice returns on gables; dormer; transom window; decorative veranda support posts, open railing

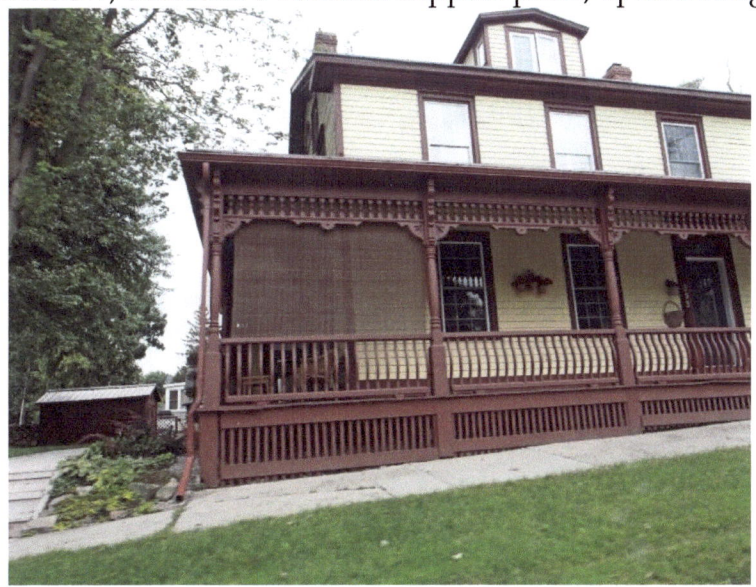

Prescott

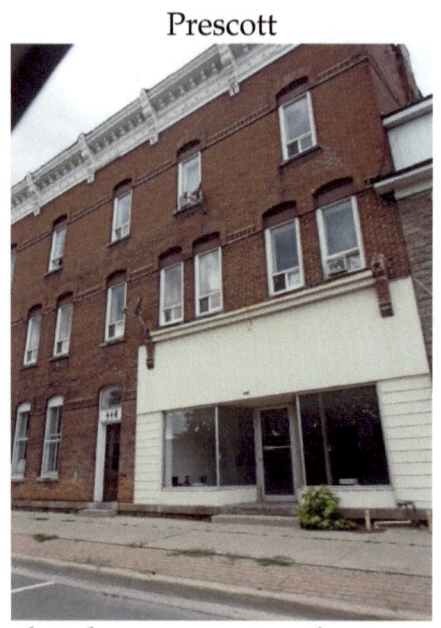

446 – cornice brackets, voussoirs, decorative brickwork

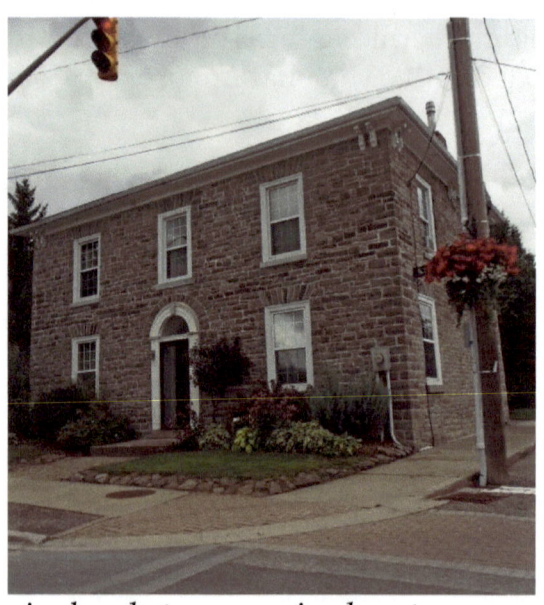

Stone, cornice brackets, voussoirs, keystone over doorway

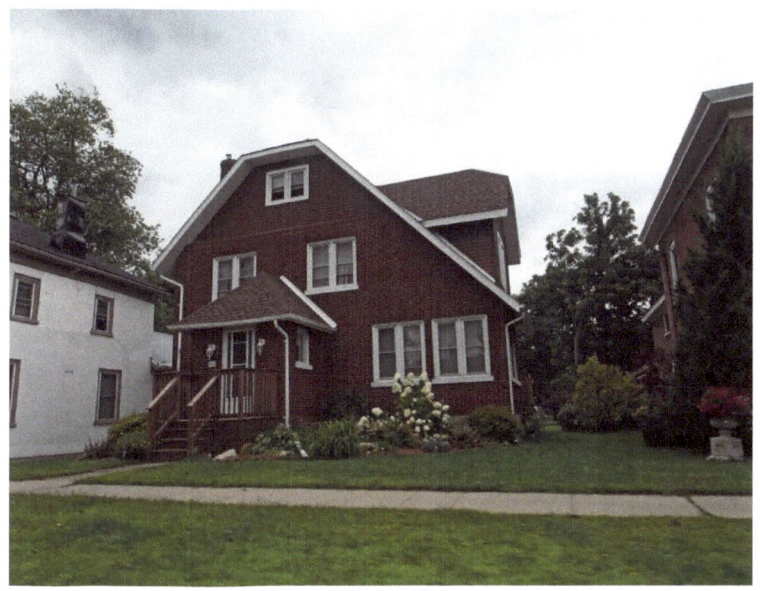

542 - Saltbox style, large dormer

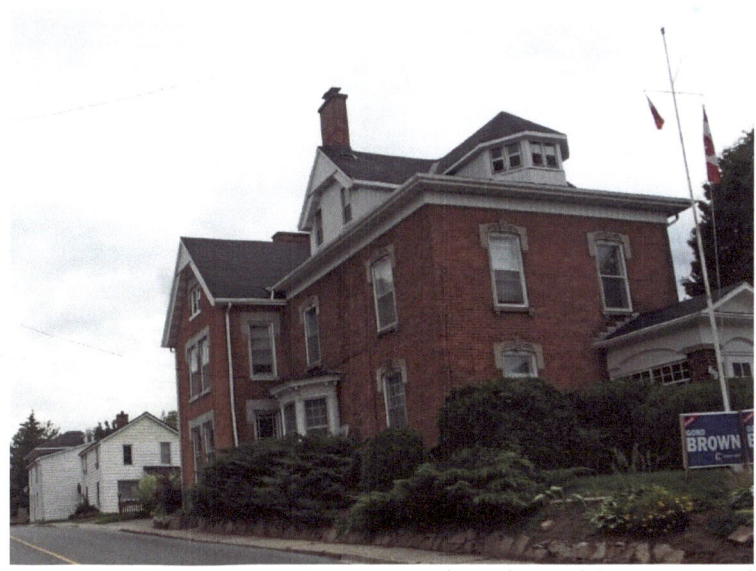

69 - dormer, belvedere, decorative lintels and keystones, bay window

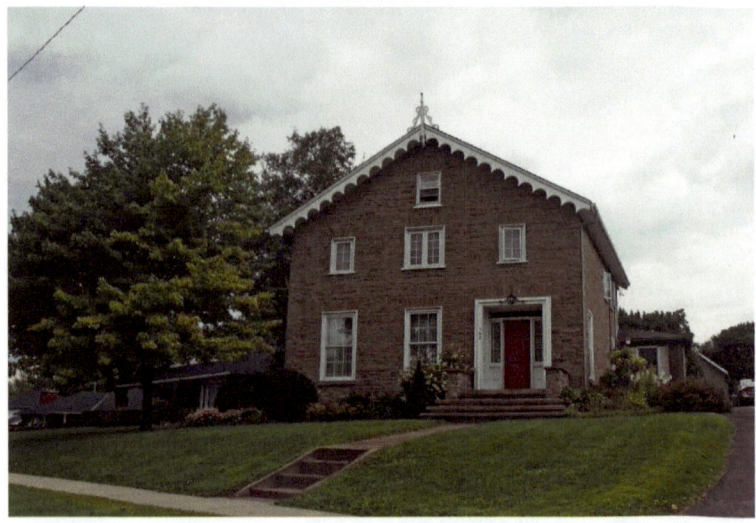

752 – Gothic – verge board trim and finial on gable, voussoirs,
sidelights and transom window

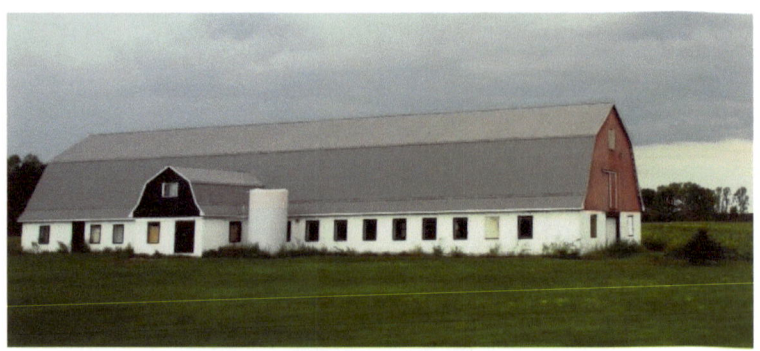

Barn with gambrel roof

Maitland

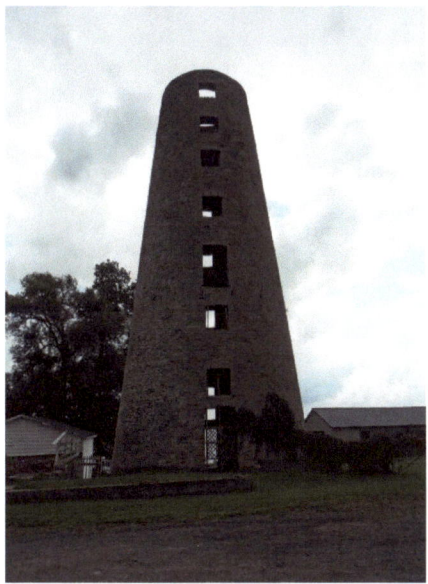

Tower

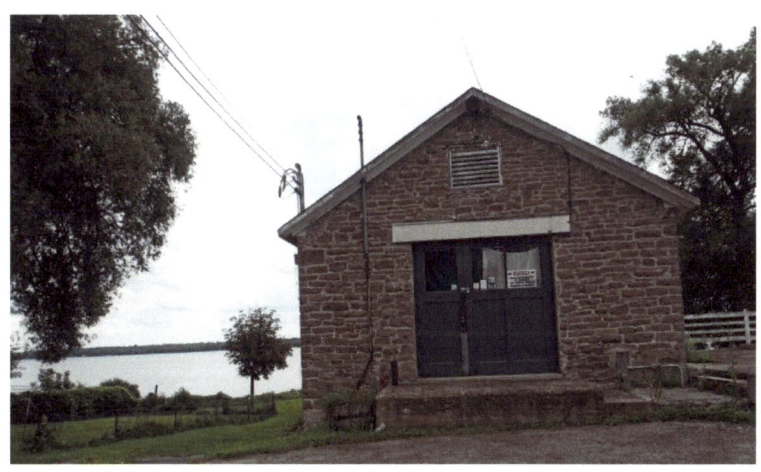

Maitland

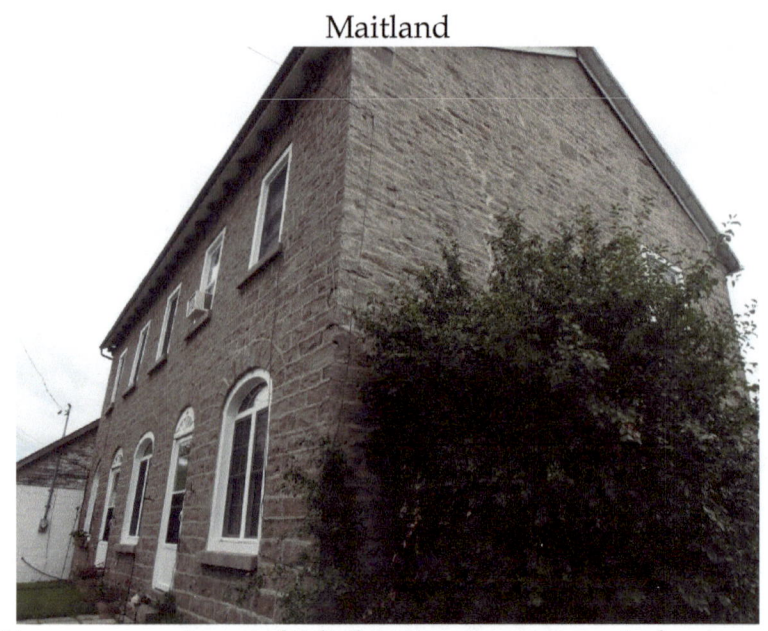

Stone, voussoirs, multi-light transoms over windows and doors

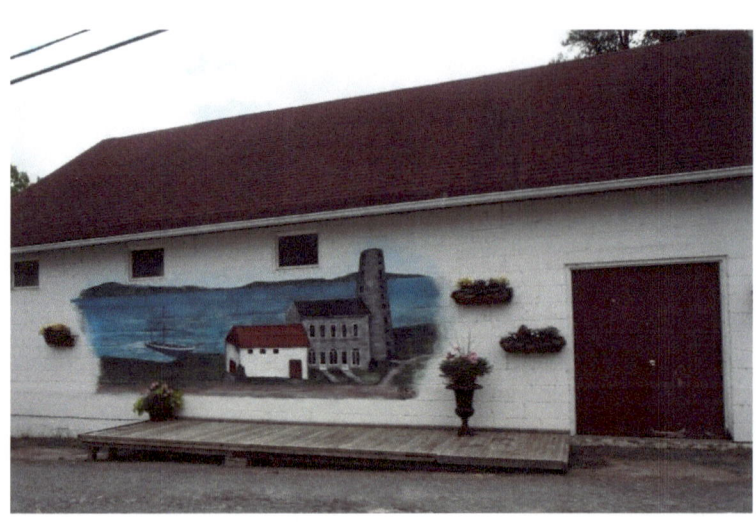

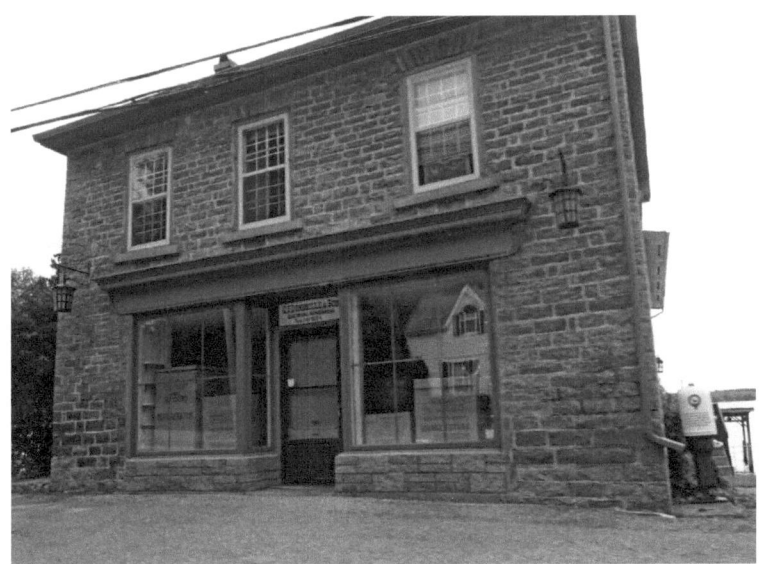

Stone

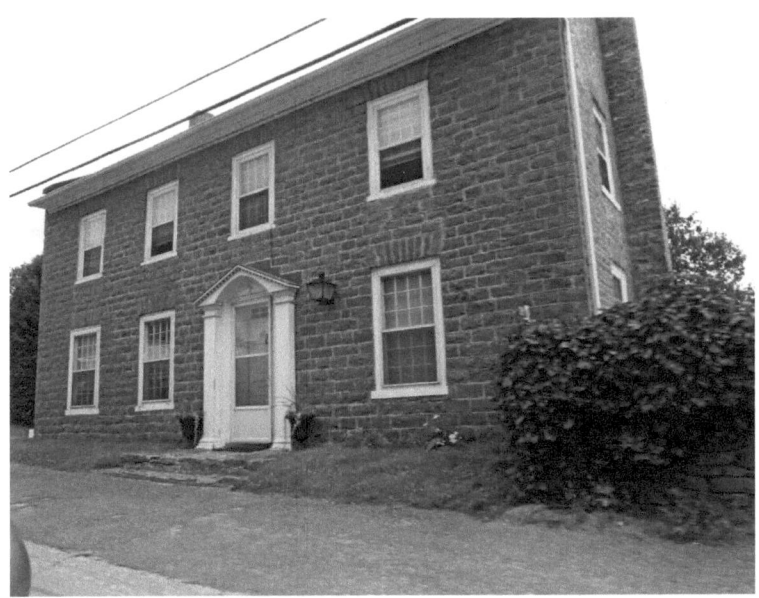

Stone, 9-over-9 sash windows, engaged columns around door

Maitland

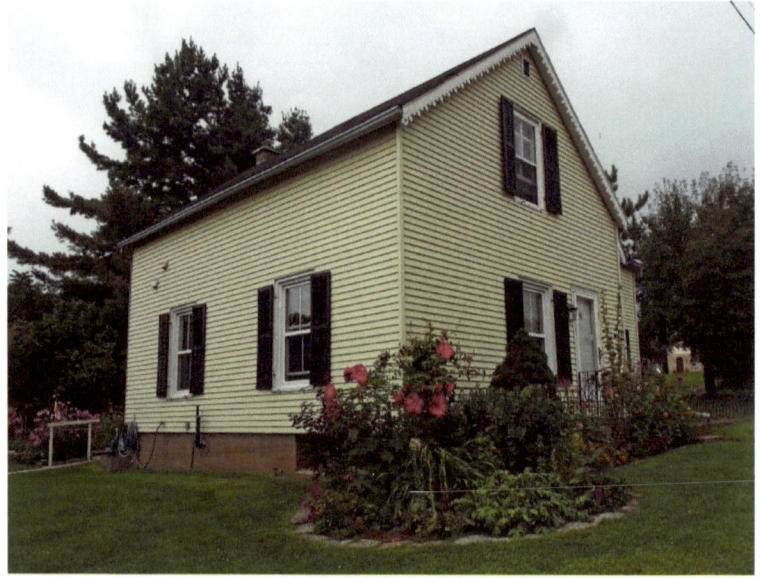

Verge board trim on gable

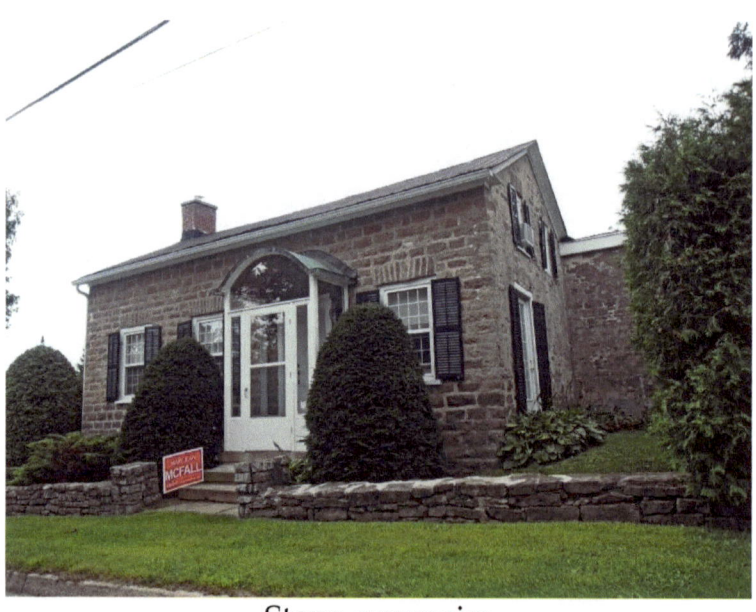

Stone, voussoirs

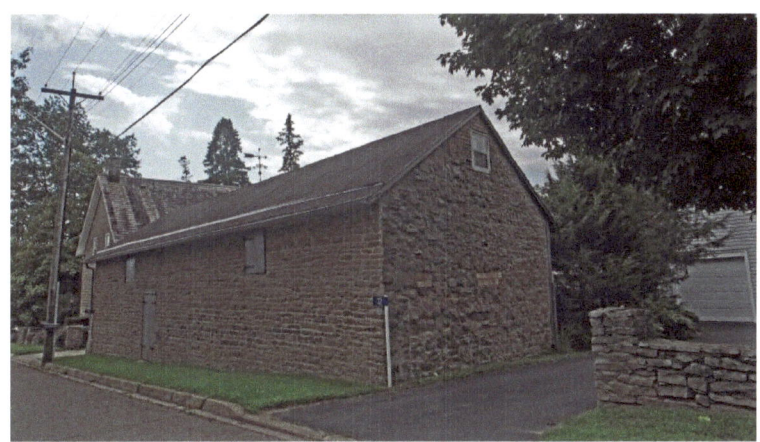

Stone

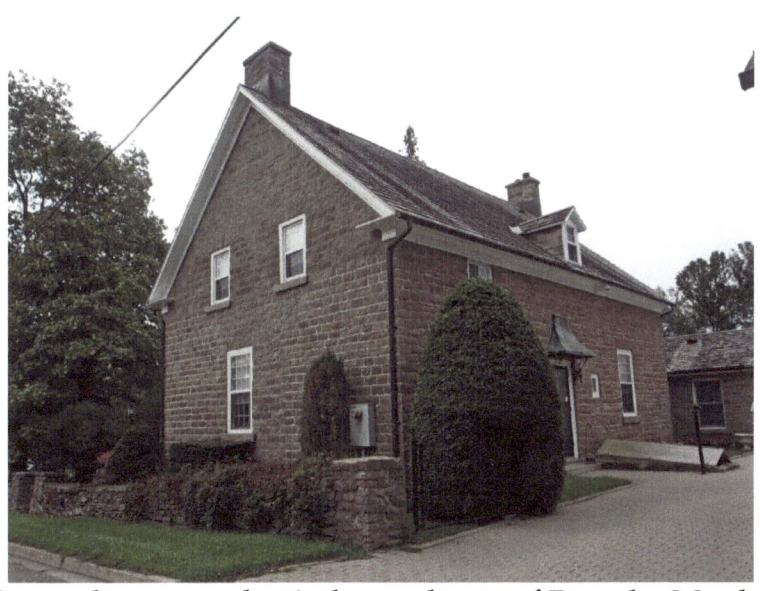

Stone, dormer, sash windows – home of Dorothy Martha Dumbrille, novelist, poet, historian, author of ten books – During World War II she wrote a novel, *All This Difference*, which addressed the tensions between the French Canadian inhabitants and the early Scots living in Glengarry County. This house, her ancestral home, was the setting of a subsequent novel, *Deep Doorways*, published in 1947.

Architectural Terms

Banding: Different materials, colors or textures used in horizontal bands along a wall. Example: St. Andrew's and St. James' Presbyterian Church, Cardinal, Page 21	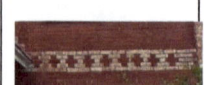
Bay Window: A window that projects out from a wall, in a semicircular, rectangular, or polygonal design. Used frequently in Gothic and Victorian designs. Example: 427 Victoria Street, Cardinal, Page 22	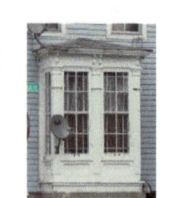
Belvedere: (from the Italian "beautiful view") an architectural feature on a roof, in a garden or on a terrace that gives a beautiful view. Example: #69, Prescott, Page 42	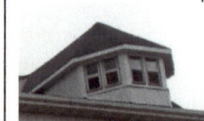
Brackets: a decorative or weight-bearing structural element which forms a right angle with one side against a wall and the other under a projecting surface such as an eave or roof. Example: Mechanics Block, Prescott, Page 29	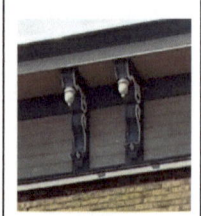
Buttress: a masonry structure built against or projecting from a wall which serves to support or reinforce the wall. In Canadian architecture, they are sometimes used for decoration. Example: St. John's Church, Cardinal, Page 22	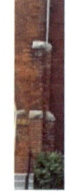

Capital: The uppermost finish or decoration on a column. A Doric column is characterized by a plain column with no base, a shaft with twenty flutings, and a simple capital with a simple entablature. Example: 363 George Street, Prescott, Page 38	
Cobblestone architecture: Refers to the use of cobblestones embedded in mortar as a method for erecting walls on houses and commercial buildings. Example: Johnstown, Page 26	
Columns were initially created to support a roof and porch structure. Originally they were free standing. Over time, builders began to build the walls between the columns so that the columns were part of the wall itself. These are called engaged columns. Engaged columns can be either structural or decorative. Example: Maitland, Page 45	
Cornice: originally the wooden overhang of the roof. With the use of stone, brick, iron and steel, the cornice is any horizontal moulded projection at the top of a building. They can be very decorative. Example: 115-123 King Street, Prescott, Page 28	
Cornice Return: decorative element on the end of a gable. Example: Mariatown, Page 12	
Dentil Moulding: an even series of rectangles used as ornamental decoration in cornices. Example: Presbyterian Church, Cardinal, Page 23	

Dichromatic brickwork: the use of two colours of brick, tile or slate to decorate a façade. Example: Presbyterian Church, Cardinal, Pg. 23	
Dormer: (French for "sleep") a gable end window that pierces through the plane of a sloping roof surface to create usable space in the top floor or attic of a building by adding headroom. Example: Mariatown, Page 15	
Gable: the triangular portion of a wall between the edges of a sloping roof. Example: Mariatown, Page 13	
Gambrel Roof: a symmetrical two-sided roof with two slopes on each side; the upper slope is positioned at a shallow angle, while the lower slope is steep. It is similar to a mansard roof, but a gambrel has vertical gable ends instead of being hipped at the four corners of the building. Example: Prescott barn, Page 42	
Hipped Roof: a roof where all sides slope downwards to the walls with no gables. Example: Mariatown, Page 16	
Iron Cresting: A decorative ornament along the top of a roof. Iron cresting was popular in the Baroque era and also in Italianate, Victorian, Second Empire and Queen Anne styles of architecture. Example: Victorian house, Cardinal, Page 21	

Keystones and Voussoirs: a voussoir is a wedge-shaped element used in building an arch. A keystone is the central stone that locks all the stones into position, allowing the arch to bear weight. A keystone is often enlarged and embellished. Example: Iroquois, Page 17	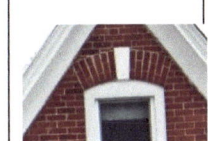
Lancet Window: a tall, narrow window with a pointed arch at its top. Example: United Church, Cardinal, Page 22	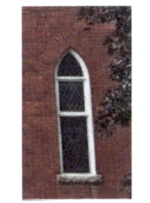
Lintel: horizontal part above a window or door that supports the structure above it. Example: Prescott, Page 41	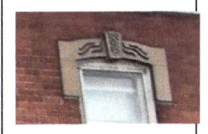
Pediment: a triangular section above the door or portico, usually supported by columns. The inside of the triangle is called the tympanum. Example: Mariatown, Page 11	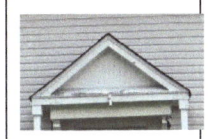
Pilaster: a slightly projecting column built into or applied to the face of a wall for additional structural support. Example: 115-123 King Street, Prescott, Page 28	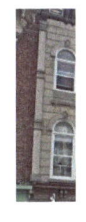

Quoin: masonry blocks at the corner of a wall, often a decorative feature, usually larger or of a different colour than the rest of the wall. Example: 490 Centre Street, Prescott, Page 35	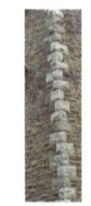
Sidelight: a vertical window that flanks a door, and is often used to emphasize the importance of a primary entrance. **Transom Window:** the light above the doorway, also called a fanlight. Example: Iroquois, Page 19	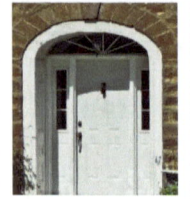
Tower: A circular, square, or octagonal vertical structure higher than the surrounding structure that is usually part of an existing building and is created either for extra defense or for a specific purpose such as a clock or a bell tower. Example: Victorian home, Cardinal, Page 21	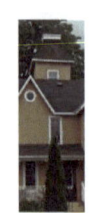
Verge board and Finial: also called bargeboards – hang from the projecting end of a roof and are often elaborately carved and ornamented. **Finial:** ornament added to the top of a gable, pinnacle, canopy or spire. Example: Prescott, Page 42	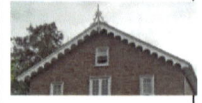
Window Hood: A **hood** is the piece found above window openings, usually of an ornate design, and covers the top third of the opening. Hoods are commonly placed above arched or curved openings on both windows and doors. Example: King Street West, Prescott, Page 30	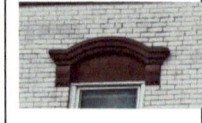

Building Styles

Georgian, before 1860 – This style began with the British King Georges in the 18th century. These buildings have balanced facades around a central door, medium-pitched gable roofs, and small paned windows. Example: 393 George Street, Prescott, Page 39	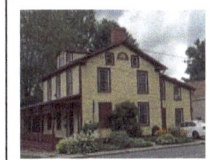
Gothic Revival, 1830-1890 – These decorative buildings have sharply-pitched gables with highly detailed verge boards, pointed-arch window openings, and dichromatic brickwork. It is a common style in Ontario. Example: Mariatown, Page 10	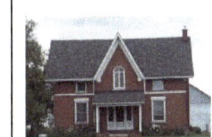
Italianate, 1850-1900 – A two story rectangular building with a mild hip roof, a projecting frontispiece, and generous eaves with ornate cornice brackets was the basis of the style; often there are large sash windows, quoins, ornate detailing on the windows, belvederes and wraparound verandahs. Italianate commercial buildings often have cast iron cresting and elegant window surrounds. Example: 115-123 King Street, Prescott, Page 28	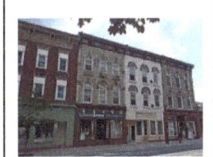
Romanesque Revival, 1880-1910 – This style hearkens back to medieval architecture of the 11th and 12th centuries with a heavy appearance, blocky towers and rounded arches. Example: 461 Centre Street, Prescott, Page 33	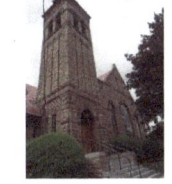

Saltbox: A saltbox is a building with a long, pitched roof that slopes down to the back, generally a wooden frame house. A saltbox has just one storey in the back and two stories in the front. The asymmetry of the unequal sides and the long, low rear roof line are the most distinctive features of a saltbox, which takes its name from its resemblance to a wooden lidded box in which salt was once kept. The earliest saltbox houses were created when a lean-to addition was added onto the rear of the original house extending the roof line sometimes to less than six feet from ground level. Example: Prescott, Page 42	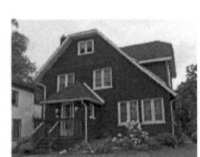
Victorian - In Ontario, a Victorian style building can be seen as any building built between 1840 and 1900 that doesn't fit into any of the other categories. It encompasses a large group of buildings constructed in brick, stone, and timber, using an eclectic mixture of Classical and Gothic motifs. Example: #2056, Cardinal, Page 21	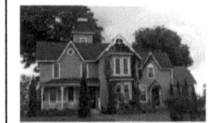